A Blueprint for Better Banking

Svenska Handelsbanken and a proven model for
more stable and profitable banking

by Niels Kroner

HARRIMAN HOUSE LTD

3A Penns Road
Petersfield
Hampshire
GU32 2EW
GREAT BRITAIN

Tel: +44 (0)1730 233870
Fax: +44 (0)1730 233880
Email: enquiries@harriman-house.com
Website: www.harriman-house.com

First published as hardback in Great Britain in 2009
This edition published in 2011

The right of Niels Kroner to be identified as the author has been asserted
in accordance with the Copyright, Design and Patents Act 1988.

978-0-857190-97-0

British Library Cataloguing in Publication Data
A CIP catalogue record for this book can be obtained from the British Library.

Printed and bound in the UK by CPI Antony Rowe, Chippenham

Contents

Table of Figures

Acknowledgements

This book would not have been possible without the many people at Handelsbanken who explained the bank's thinking to me. In particular, I would like to express my gratitude to Pär Boman, Ulf Riese, Thommy Mossinger, Magnus Uggla, Olle Lindstrand, Bengt Edholm, Mikael Hallåker, Lars Kenneth Dahlqvist, and Bengt Ragnå. They all found time for numerous in-depth discussions with me when they had to manage the bank through the financial crisis. Rosina Galvin and Terry Blacker at Handelsbanken London deserve credit for demonstrating to me as a customer how the Handelsbanken model works in practice.

Many colleagues and friends have provided me with valuable comments, as have fellow members of the Worshipful Company of International Bankers. I am deeply grateful to them. Some of the ideas in this book were first aired by me at a panel discussion organised by Somerville College, Oxford, and I would like to thank my fellow panellists as well as a very lively audience for intriguing comments and questions. In addition, I am very grateful to my editors, Stephen Eckett at Harriman House and Peter Chambers, for their enthusiasm and constructive feedback. I am indebted to Sylvain Marpeau-Roussel and Julia Hofmann for their input. I would also like to thank Cornelius Walter for his continued support, as well as Gorm Thomassen and Nicolai Tangen. My very special thanks go to Fabian Eser at Nuffield College, Oxford. His thorough review of the manuscript and his penetrating questions caused me sleepless nights but ultimately helped to make this book much better than it would have been without his invaluable support.

Niels Kroner, London, 2009

Foreword

Almost every day there is a new publication on the financial crisis. The media offer us a host of general and specific explanations of what went wrong and why, who is to blame and, of course, what should be done to avoid similar turmoil in future. It can come as no surprise that there is a variety of schools of thought often based on different scientific or political backgrounds and intentions. Consequently we are offered a wide array of perceived causes, culprits and macroeconomic and political mistakes. The non-professional consumer of such news is confused and made to believe that in some way or another all important financial institutions are involved and that, apart from good luck, a bank cannot protect itself in the long term against the pitfalls of imprudent banking.

Niels Kroner has discovered a bank that can do just that: Svenska Handelsbanken. Today, having mastered not only the present problems but also the Swedish banking crisis in the early 1990s, the bank's market capitalisation puts it among the top 25 in Europe.

The author, with his intimate knowledge of the financial markets, shows us how Handelsbanken was able to avoid the temptations of the "seven deadly sins" that he lists in the first part of this book.

Having been at the helm of a European bank with a sizeable retail network, a wide corporate client base and aspiring to become one of the leading global investment banks, I am fully aware how demanding it is to sustain Handelsbanken's strategy, its operational model and its culture. This is particularly true at periods when, to use Keynes' famous words, 'animal spirits' seem to have had an unparalleled impact on bankers, depositors and borrowers. Maybe regulators should be included for good measure.

I enjoyed and benefited from reading Niels Kroner's book. His general view of the present crisis and its main causes, and his knowledgeable portrayal of Handelsbanken's non-involvement for the second time in 20 years in a severe financial crisis, is most informative. It may help readers to avoid making similar mistakes in future.

Hilmar Kopper, Frankfurt, May 2009

Former chairman and CEO of Deutsche Bank.
Former trustee of the International Accounting Standards Committee.
Chairman designate of HSH Nordbank.

Introduction

Over the past two years we have seen spectacular failures and bail-outs of financial institutions. These have been all the more dramatic because, until early 2007, many of them were among those with the highest market capitalisation and seemed the most solid, successful organisations. The effects of their implosion, far from being limited to the financial sector, have engulfed entire economies in the developed and the developing world.

Given these developments it is understandable that many people ask why the financial crisis happened and what needs to be done to avoid a similar breakdown of our financial system in the future. There are very thoughtful general explanations of the first question, ranging from those that blame macroeconomic factors and policy mistakes – especially in setting interest rates – to those that identify psychology and behavioural issues, in the widest sense, as the primary causes.

When it comes to describing how individual banks and financial institutions failed, however, these explanations are all unsatisfactory. Since they are generalised, they portray banks that failed largely as victims: be it of unfortunate macroeconomic trends, policies, or shortcomings of human understanding and behaviour. Their accounts, therefore, are very difficult to square with the often lurid and sensational descriptions of individual banks running into trouble. General explanations of the credit crunch can thus only ever be half the story.

On the other hand, we are offered a plethora of bank-specific explanations of what went wrong and what should be changed in the future. We hear that the cause of the crisis was the bonus culture, light-touch regulation, a short-term focus on shareholder value creation, or the combination of commercial and investment banking which allowed risk-seeking investment bankers literally to bet the bank. Their advantage over general explanations is that they answer more convincingly not just what went wrong in the abstract but very specifically what banks did wrong. As a result these explanations lead more easily to answers to the second question: what should be changed.

Yet the challenge for all bank-specific explanations is that each of them works only for a subset of failed institutions. The long list of financial institutions that disappeared or had to be bailed out includes those with high bonuses and those without, lightly and heavily regulated ones, those with and without a shareholder value focus, commercial banks as well as investment banks as well as those that are both. As a consequence, each bank-specific explanation is inadequate.

So how can we find an explanation that is comprehensive while at the same time addressing where the banks went wrong?

The Seven Deadly Sins of Imprudent Banking

My main argument on this front will be that there are seven types of activities or behaviours sufficiently widespread among banks so as to often cause both individual *and* systemic crises. They are widespread because they can be profitable in the short to medium term – which is why bank executives are tempted by them and often pressed by their shareholders to pursue them. At the same time they are imprudent: they can lead to large losses eventually. I will call these types of behaviour the seven deadly sins.

I will describe these deadly sins and show the many times they have caused financial crises in the past. I will also try to explain why financial institutions are so susceptible to them. The seven deadly sins usually appear attractive and profitable in those macroeconomic environments that are now taking the blame in some of the general explanations for the credit crunch. The seven deadly sins thus link the general explanations with an account of what went wrong in individual institutions.

More Saintly Banking

The core part of this book, and the more interesting one for the question of how we should redesign our financial institutions, will be a description of a fairly large bank that has avoided most of the pitfalls of the credit crunch. It is today arguably in a stronger position than ever before. Svenska Handelsbanken, the largest bank in Sweden, is well known for being the only bank that survived the Swedish banking crisis in 1991/2 without having to approach the government for support or tapping its owners for emergency capital injections. While other banks had to be nationalised, Handelsbanken came out of the crisis with net income 50% higher than its pre-crisis record year.

Hundreds of papers have been written about the Swedish banking crisis in general. But strangely, nobody has investigated what this one bank did differently. Today, Handelsbanken looks well on course for repeating this performance in the current financial crisis. It is all the more surprising, therefore, that the ingredients of Handelsbanken's model are not more widely known.

Handelsbanken sounds much less familiar than other banking brand names, in part because the bank does hardly any advertising. Yet at the end of April 2009 its market capitalisation of EUR 9 billion easily placed the bank among the 25 biggest in Europe, on par with Lloyds, which had once been the world's most valuable bank. Handelsbanken's share price had significantly outperformed the industry.

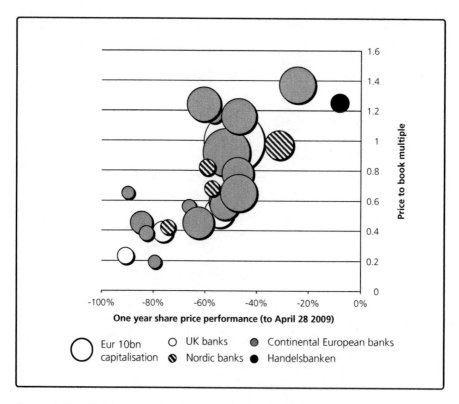

Figure 1: Top 25 European banks by market capitalisation

One standard measure of a bank's valuation is its price to book multiple, and on this Handelsbanken was among the most highly valued banks in Europe. (See Figure 1 above.)

In addition, Handelsbanken has a stabilising effect on the economy as it continues to lend to corporate and household customers. It is also a net borrower to the banking system and the Swedish state.

When I talked about Handelsbanken with bankers, analysts or institutional investors, they usually characterised them, in a more or less dismissive way, as 'odd', 'very old-fashioned' or, my favourite, as just 'losing it'. In the description of its peers, Handelsbanken was the banking industry's ugly duckling.

Given their impressive survival track record and the unanimous belief that 'Handelsbanken is very different' it is surprising that there has been so little interest in understanding the Handelsbanken way of managing a bank.

My interest is not in a detailed historical description of Handelsbanken. Rather, I am interested in their management model to the extent that managers at other banks (or governments as the lucky new owners of banks that need to be restructured) can

> **Given their impressive survival track record it is surprising that there has been so little interest in understanding the Handelsbanken way.**

learn from them. Describing the way they work is interesting for our purposes only insofar as it helps us understand what "better banking" would look like.

Handelsbanken does not always succeed in living up to its management philosophy, of course. But having a real-life illustration of a sound banking model is far more useful than coming up with abstract designs for post-credit crunch banking, for two reasons.

The first is that the real life profile will be richer and informed by decades of experience. Many details turn out to be important but are easy to overlook when one outlines a prudent bank in theory. The second reason is simply that with any abstract blueprint one can argue *ad nauseam* whether it works or not. Having a real life example that has been operating successfully for many years takes away this problem.

How Handelsbanken Works

Hence the second and main part of this book will describe the Handelsbanken model in five different chapters.

The first of these (Chapter 4) will give a brief overview of its history and its activities today.

Chapter 5 will then will analyse the way Handelsbanken thinks about strategy and how this automatically avoids the temptation of some of the seven deadly sins for fast profit growth. It will, in particular, focus on the way Handelsbanken manages its business by giving branches a high degree of autonomy. In addition, we will discuss how its strategy is led by considerations of what the bank is really good at, rather than by analyses about where most money can be made.

Chapter 6 will look at Handelsbanken's incentive system and the bank's values system, which are both rather different from its peers'. Given the intense current debates about bankers' bonuses it is interesting to see that one can motivate staff without any bonuses – by means of friendly internal competition and entrepreneurial freedom alone. The idea that the best and brightest will work for banks only if

> " Seeing a bank that works rather well without bonuses may be a bit like the financial world's "black swan event". "

there are substantial financial rewards for success is second nature to people working in the industry. I doubt whether most teachers, doctors or artists would ever have agreed. So seeing a bank that works rather well without bonuses may be a bit like the financial world's "black swan event" (i.e. an event that sounds so unthinkable that nobody expected it).

My comments on Handelsbanken's culture are inevitably rather more impressionistic, and in this chapter I have drawn more heavily on my personal observations from nearly fifty interviews with bank staff.

The following chapter (Chapter 7) will then outline Handelsbanken's approach to risk management, especially some guiding principles about what types of risk the bank should and should not incur. It will also describe their risk organisation and how it, too, functions as a defence against engaging in imprudent activities for short-term gains.

Finally, Chapter 8 will describe the way the bank interacts with its investors. It will discuss how Handelsbanken has created a firewall against the investor pressure for steadily growing profits that would otherwise lead to imprudent activities.

Following this, Chapter 9 will close with an assessment of how much this all really matters. To what extent does being a different bank really make Handelsbanken a better bank in the eyes of customers and shareholders? It will also discuss things that may not be perfect at Handelsbanken – a reminder that this book is about what they can teach us even if they themselves do not follow their own precepts all the time.

In a sense there is nothing brilliant or revolutionary about Handelsbanken – it is just good banking, prudent and well run, and there may well be hundreds of smaller institutions run along similar lines. Older bankers I have talked to told me that large banks in the 1950s and 1960s shared many elements of the current Handelsbanken approach. But today most large banks are run on a very different basis, and the Handelsbanken example is of interest because it shows that prudent ideas of good banking still work well in the 21st century and on the scale of a very large bank.

Implications

The third part of this book discusses what it all means, i.e. what other banks can learn from Handelsbanken and what its example implies for regulators. Even if one accepts that Handelsbanken is a well-managed bank run along very different principles, one may be sceptical about their model being transferable to any other institution. Hence I shall argue that their model can (and actually does) work well outside Sweden and that it can be applied to a broad range of banking activities.

Handelsbanken's experience also casts doubt on the regulatory response to the financial crisis. If a large universal bank does well and actually provides credit when few other banks do, it is debatable whether better regulation should start with penal capital charges on large institutions or with a separation of commercial and investment banking. Hence this chapter will also suggest rather different regulatory priorities based on the analysis of the seven deadly sins and the Handelsbanken example.

About the Author

In my professional career I have been a management consultant for a number of banks, worked for a UK clearing bank, and worked as an institutional investor and buy side analyst in the banking sector. But I have never worked for Handelsbanken itself.

This is in fact something of an advantage: the Handelsbanken example becomes truly interesting only when set against the management practices at other banks. Since Handelsbanken staff today have usually been with the bank for many years, they tend not to see the revealing differences. One former chief executive, Jan Wallander, wrote a book that emphasises the commitment to decentralisation and low costs. But it does not bring out the equally important differences in Handelsbanken's approach to risk management, strategy formulation and capital markets communication. Perhaps Handelsbanken insiders do not even realise how different they are and that they might have the solutions to a number of problems other banks are facing.

In that sense writing this book feels a bit like being an ethnographer observing a very different people. The ethnographer will be less intimate with the culture he describes than they themselves are, but he will perhaps be in a better position to contextualise, comprehend and explain that culture to others. What he lacks in inside experience is offset by impartiality, and his outsider's position in fact provides the somewhat removed perspective that enables him to better apprehend the essential features and differences of that culture.

My research and analysis into Handelsbanken has been extensive; the nearly fifty interviews I have conducted with Handelsbanken staff have included senior executives, branch managers and staff. As a result, I am confident that I know the Handelsbanken way thoroughly – whilst also having first hand experience with a wide array of other European banks to bring out the contrast between the two approaches.

Whilst Handelsbanken have been very helpful in providing useful information, they had no influence over my writing of this book. And apart from the fact that it is of course nice that you are purchasing a book I have written about them, I have no economic interest whatsoever in the bank.

Part I

Explanations for the Financial Crisis

1

General Explanations

Explanations for the cause of the credit crunch fall into two big families.

On one side are those that seek its cause in the background on which the financial system has been operating – the **general explanations**. On the other side are **bank-specific explanations** that identify as the culprit characteristics or particular activities of the banking system.

General explanations themselves fall into three camps.

Macro Explanations

The first, *macro explanations*, blames mostly macroeconomic imbalances such as large current account deficits in the US, UK, Ireland, Spain and similar economies, and large current account surpluses financing them in the large exporting countries (China, Germany, Japan, oil-producing nations). According to this theory, sometimes referred to as the "savings glut explanation", the desire of surplus countries to invest in risk free fixed income instruments has decreased real interest rates to historically low levels. This has, via credit expansion, caused asset bubbles, especially in housing markets, and driven investors who require a certain yield to invest in structured credit products that promised safety as well as a small yield pick up. Rising house prices and low volatility have then boosted the value of financial instruments based on housing assets. The banks engaged in structuring credit, therefore, have been able to generate high and stable profits leading them to believe that they are doing the right thing and that they can operate with high capital leverage.

The "savings glut" concept was developed by Ben Bernanke in 2005.[1] It was linked to the financial crisis more recently by, amongst others, Paul Krugman and Adair Turner, the chairman of the UK's Financial Services Authority (FSA).

Policy Mistake Explanations

The second, *policy mistake* camp, disputes the empirical evidence for the savings glut theory and blames misguided central bank policy, especially in the US, for abnormally low interest rates. Keeping interest rates intentionally lower than would be warranted is seen as a policy decision to deal with the aftermath of the dotcom boom and to avoid the Japanese experience with deflation. Its unintended consequence was a housing boom (and later bust) which, short term, benefited in particular subprime lending.

Adherents of the policy mistake theory also see government decisions to tackle the financial crisis as largely unrelated to the real problems, instead creating new complications as unintended consequences. The real problem is essentially a solvency crisis which the government fights with liquidity injections and tax reliefs that have no effect.

It is quite ironic that the policy mistake school includes two very different warring camps in economics. It is home to defenders of the efficient market hypothesis, who believe financial markets are inherently stable and destabilisation comes from government and central bank intervention. One of its most thoughtful proponents is the Stanford economist John Taylor. But the policy mistake school also includes the camp that believes financial markets are by nature unstable and need governments and central banks as a counteracting force and shock

---

[1] "The Global Saving Glut and the U.S. Current Account Deficit", speech on March 10th, 2005.

absorber. In this view, misguided policies have amplified the instability of financial markets, leading to the current crisis.

The policy mistake school can thus count Friedman as well as Keynes and Minsky among its ancestors. Building on Keynes, Minsky's framework is a combination of the policy error and the behavioural approach, though the former aspect of his work receives less attention. Minsky's explanation of increased financial instability in the second half of the 20th century refers to an interventionist big government that acts as lender of last resort and bails out financial institutions while mitigating the recession following any financial crisis by a surge in public spending.[2] Minsky sees some legitimacy in a public policy trade-off between infrequent deep recessions and frequent financial crises with moderate recessions. However, he is critical of governments that are interventionist during crises but revert to a laissez-faire attitude afterwards. They thus fail to take any steps to deal with inflationary pressures and an accident prone financial system operating on ever thinner safety margins.

Behavioural Explanations

The third group, *behavioural explanations*, is based on the belief that "the subprime crisis was essentially psychological in origin, as are all bubbles". It looks for an explanation for the credit crunch in deviations of actual human nature from an idealised *homo economicus*.[3] Proponents include Robert Shiller and George Akerlof, whose work is

---

[2] Minksy's view is frequently taken as identical to Kindleberger's monetarist explanation ("Kindleberger-Minsky model"). In fact, there are tensions between them about whether financial crises have changed in nature in the second half of the 19th century and about the role of a lender of last resort.

[3] Shiller (2008), p. 24.

founded on behavioural finance; and one would also have to include George Soros and his concept of reflexivity. But long before behavioural finance was invented similar accounts could be found in the writings of John Stuart Mill, Charles Mackay, François Juglar and, one and a half centuries later, John Kenneth Galbraith. As mentioned before, Hyman Minsky's work includes behavioural explanations; we will come back to them.

But This is Not Enough

The explanations proffered by the macro imbalances, the policy error and the behavioural schools are intellectually extremely stimulating and well researched. But they all have great difficulty in explaining the developments leading to the financial crisis in microeconomic terms. It is unlikely that any participant in the decision-making of a specific bank would recognise in the macro explanations what he or she has witnessed. It is simply not what an insider saw really happening, hence the disconnect between general explanations and descriptions of events at failed banks.[4]

There is a strong presumption that banks collectively have made a number of mistakes that have contributed materially to the current situation. Part of the problem is that general explanations by definition assign at best a supporting role to banks themselves; they can easily

---

[4] For instance Cohan (2009) on Bear Stearns or Walters (2008) on Northern Rock. More sensationalist titles that blame recklessness and greed include Richard Bitner: *Confessions of a Subprime Lender: An Insider's Tale of Greed, Fraud, and Ignorance*; Philip Augar: *Chasing Alpha, How Reckless Growth and Unchecked Ambition Ruined the City's Golden Decade*, and Alex Brummer: *The Crunch: How Greed and Incompetence Sparked the Credit Crisis*. The titles say it all.

appear to become victims of developments outside their control.[5] This, however, is not plausible. Nor does it explain the vast differences between institutions even in very similar markets.

This is not to say that general explanations are wrong – merely that they are incomplete. They need to be combined with an analysis of why banks were so susceptible to the factors described and why they were apparently happy to maintain or increase their exposure. This element is necessary for a satisfactory explanation – and to answer the question on how the banking system should be redesigned. Bank executives and regulators are hardly in a position to change macro imbalances, policy mistakes or human nature.

---

[5] Which is a role eagerly accepted by bankers. See for instance the ad hoc announcement by the CEO of Northern Rock after it had to seek emergency support from the Bank of England: 'we have done nothing wrong [...] we are literally victims of a global financial crisis.' (London Stock Exchange, September 14th, 2007).

2

Bank-Specific Explanations

Plenty of bank-specific explanations have been brought forth that avoid the difficulties of general explanations. They capture mistakes within banks that an inside observer would recognise. As they address specifically what went wrong in these institutions they lead quite easily to recommendations on how banking should be different in the future.

The main problem for all specific explanations is that they apply only to a subset of institutions that have run into trouble. For every alleged evil there are scores of banks that have done the exact opposite and still become victims of the credit crunch.

There are five main groups of bank-specific issues that are blamed for the crisis:

1) excessive and asymmetric bonus systems,

2) short-term orientation towards shareholder value,

3) repeal of the Glass-Steagall Act which separated investment or "casino" banking from commercial or "utility" banking,

4) lax, light-touch regulation, and

5) misguided accounting standards and capital guidelines.

Big Bonuses

Paying bankers a big bonus in good times, so the argument goes, skims off profits while losses in bad years accrue fully to shareholders. Similarly, hedge fund investors take quite a big share of profits, if there are any, while not sharing in losses. This gives them an incentive to gamble and "bet the bank" since they win if things go well but they do not lose if things go badly. In addition, a lot of pay does not seem sufficiently linked to performance. Bankers (as well as hedge funds or private equity investors who charge several per cent of the assets they manage regardless of performance) get paid "obscene" sums even when their institutions lose staggering amounts of money.

To be just to the incentive explanation of the credit crunch, there is indeed something seriously amiss with these incentive structures. Nevertheless, quite a number of "victims" of the credit crunch did not really have a culture of big skewed bonuses. Spanish savings banks (cajas) find themselves with a high burden of loans to property developers that are unlikely to repay their debt. The financial crisis has found victims among friendly societies in the UK, mutual banks in France, small Norwegian savings banks and Germany's IKB or state-owned Landesbanken. A German newspaper described the business habits at one of them, Bayrische Landesbank, in such devastating detail that one struggles to see how the best of Wall Street could have been worse.[6] Neither were substantial bonuses the root cause of the problems of Northern Rock.

In the US, there were even cases where management had quite a lot of their own money at stake. Lehman chairman Dick Fuld lost a large part of his fortune when Lehman went into administration, and executives at nearly all publicly listed banks lost substantial amounts of their own money when share prices plummeted.

---

[6] "Der Staat als Retter? Ausgerechnet der Staat?", *Süddeutsche Zeitung Magazin* 49/2008.

Its main point is that politicians representing the state as the bank owner directed substantial funds of the bank to non-economic purposes (loans to marginal constituencies or large-scale sponsorship of political pet projects) while being incompetent at supervising the ongoing business. One politician refused to serve on the board as he had no banking experience but was informed that the law stipulated it. Other board members dozed off or read the newspaper during board meetings, so they did not even notice when the bank became a large player in US mortgage backed securities.

Blaming bonuses is too simplistic as an explanation for the credit crunch. Wrong incentives as well as a wrong company culture play a very important role in aiding and abetting the seven deadly sins, but the relationship is more complex, and we shall discuss it in greater detail in the chapter on Handelsbanken's culture and incentives.

Shareholder Value Orientation as the Culprit?

A similar argument blames shareholder value orientation, or rather the pressure from capital markets for high quarterly profits. When describing Handelsbanken's capital markets communication, we will see that investors share part of the blame for pushing banks to do things which in hindsight they should not have done. But publicly owned banks (Sachsen LB, IKB) or banks with strong core shareholders that did not face similar pressure (Raiffeisen International, Erste Bank, SEB, Swedbank all of whom got into trouble in Eastern Europe, and arguably even AIG because of its large inside shareholders) did not avoid the credit crunch.

Bring Back Glass-Steagall!

Another explanation sees the amalgamation of investment banks and commercial banks as the main problem. Commercial banking with its basic functions of taking deposits, making loans and processing payments, according to this argument, is of great importance to the economy so there is an implicit or explicit guarantee that the government will bail it out. Commercial banking should really operate like a utility – heavily regulated and rather boring but safe.[7] Investment

---

[7] The terms "utility banking" and "casino banking" were coined by the economist and journalist Martin Wolf in a public discussion with John Kay on September 9th, 2008. They were not defined precisely but it is clear from the context that the spirit of utility banking is to operate the payment system and deposit taking like a public utility: with a low risk profile, a subordinated profit (cont.)

banking, on the other hand, does not have the same social necessity. Individual firms may benefit from speculative trading and mergers and acquisitions – but these activities do not have the same fundamental social utility as the transformation of savings into investments. Investment banking is more like many other industries. So there is no need for governments to step in if things go wrong on this "casino" side of banking.

By grafting investment banks onto commercial banks to form large universal banks, the casino is benefiting from the more stable earnings, better rating and customer funding of the utility. One subsidises investment banking and gives them a free "get out of jail" card since the government needs to bail out the entire bank if its investment banking arm implodes. So proponents of this explanation argue that the original sin was repealing the Glass-Steagall Act, which was introduced in the US in the wake of the Great Depression to separate commercial banking and investment banking.[8]

As we shall see in the second part, there is certainly something to be said about this explanation to the extent that Handelsbanken resembles the description of a utility bank rather well. Yet the identification of investment banking with casino banking and commercial banking with utility banking is again too simplistic. Handelsbanken successfully operates a low-risk investment bank, which we will describe in more detail later. And one cannot overlook that many pure commercial banks

---

motive and heavy regulation. Utility banking, because of its high importance for the entire economy, would have a government guarantee. Other activities would be left to casino banks which would be left free to do what they want but would not be bailed out.

[8] At least historically these calls are misleading. Glass-Steagall was mainly concerned with conflicts of interest of institutions underwriting securities which they would then sell on to their (retail) customers, partly on credit of up to 90% of stock purchase prices. This conflict of interest has survived in pure investment banks and their selling of toxic assets to naïve institutional investors.

and pure investment banks failed even before the large universal banks started to suffer. Northern Rock, IKB, Hypo Real Estate, Washington Mutual, Countrywide and the Irish banks were pure commercial banks that still managed to run into trouble.

Proponents of a new Glass-Steagall Act often imply that problems from "toxic" structured credit products occurred in banks' proprietary trading operations, i.e. pure investment banking, when in fact in many cases they materialised in treasury operations which every commercial bank has as well. Fortis fell apart primarily from overstretch after acquiring part of ABN Amro, not because of problems in investment banking. Fannie Mae and Freddie Mac, rather clear-cut examples of utility banks, were not saved by their absence of investment banking operations. Similarly, Dexia's problems may have come from its wholesale banking side, but it was a credit insurer and also very like a utility bank.

On the other hand, Merrill Lynch, Bear Stearns and Lehman were pure investment banks that did not have a commercial bank and its promise of implicit government support to rely on. In fact, Lehman's insolvency unveiled how many pure commercial banks had exposure to Lehman as interbank lenders or swap counterparties. This makes it difficult to argue that with a clear separation of utility banking from casino banking one could simply let failed casino banks go under. Doing exactly that in the case of Lehman has arguably not had a healthy effect on the overall banking system.

We Told You So: It's All Because of Lax Regulation

Was light-touch regulation to blame? It has become extremely popular, especially in continental Europe and on the political left, to single out lax, Anglo-Saxon regulation as the main reason for the credit crunch.

There is some truth in the argument but it is unlikely to be the main culprit since the most tightly regulated institutions such as Fannie Mae or Freddie Mac, or even AIG, did not fare much better than the lightly regulated investment banks. Institutions in very different regulatory regimes have all failed. Politicians in continental Europe who are among the most scathing critics of Anglo-Saxon regulation conveniently overlook that banks under their jurisdiction have suffered large losses as well. So it is very hard to single out any particular regulatory regime as the cause of the credit crunch. However, there is certainly agreement that regulation has failed and that it needs to be revised fundamentally to avoid the next financial crisis. We shall come back to this point in the third part of this book.

Accounting Standards Caused the Crunch

There have been arguments to reintroduce counter-cyclical provisions, i.e. forcing banks to build provisions in good times that they can then use up in bad times. It is true that prevailing accounting regimes have reduced discretion in estimating provisions since they were demonstrably used to manage earnings. Banks were, however, always free to retain (taxed) profits if they thought such a capital cushion was required for more difficult times ahead.

Accounting standards never put any pressure on banks to reduce their capitalisation; investors did. The Bank of Spain has imposed counter-cyclical provisioning on Spanish banks and the Spanish banking system has often been cited as one of the most robust as a result. This system, however, has not prevented a housing boom and now bust. It remains to be seen how solvent Spanish banks are when non-performing loans reach their peak; given that Spain has only seen the beginning of a big housing bubble bursting and given that most Spanish banks have already used up the extra cushion of reserves, it is by no means a foregone conclusion that counter-cyclical provisions are a panacea.

Even if counter-cyclical provisions may work for very traditional credit cycles it is doubtful if they would have made any difference to all the problem areas that have brought financial institutions into disarray. Many of them (liquidity risks, holding "toxic securities" or large-scale writing of credit default swaps) had no meaningful capital requirements in the first place, so pro-cyclical requirements would not have changed much. And one should not forget that, prior to US GAAP and IFRS[9] clamp-downs on discretionary loan loss provisioning, banks did by and large build counter-cyclical loan loss reserves. This did not prevent the many previous banking crises.

In my opinion it is similarly a stretch to blame the Basel II regulation for leaving banks weakly capitalised in a downturn. Under Basel II the counter-cyclical "through the cycle" measurement of risk weights is the preferred methodology – although "point in time" approaches are tolerated which may assign low capital requirements to loans in good times.[10] But it is an exaggeration to claim that Basel II itself is pro-cyclical when its preferred model is precisely the opposite. In addition, Basel II explicitly gives regulators the tool, via stress testing capital levels under the so-called pillar II, to impose higher capital requirements on

---

[9] US Generally Accepted Accounting Principles (US GAAP) are the mandatory accounting standards for companies listed on US stock exchanges. Most companies outside the US follow International Financial Reporting Standards (IFRS). Both US GAAP and IFRS have strict criteria for loan loss provisions; they rule out making provisions for loan losses that are expected in the future but have not yet materialised.

[10] More specifically, the Basel accord (Part 2, II, H, 3, iv) requires that banks' estimates of a borrower's default are based on a longer time horizon. The accord states that the assessment should be conservative, possibly including a stress test for conditions that are likely over the business cycle. This might be vague. But the claim that Basel II encourages risk assessments that are too optimistic in good times does not stand up to scrutiny. See Jeremy Taylor: "Risk-Grading Philosophy: Through the Cycle versus Point in Time", in: The RMA Journal 86 (2003), pp. 32-47.

banks that are sensitive to deteriorations in their environment. If regulators have not used these tools properly one cannot blame the Basel framework.

Accounting standards play an important role in connection with the seven deadly sins, which we will discuss in the next chapter. But the view that they are the cause of the financial crisis is hard to defend.

3

Banks' Seven Deadly Sins

The missing link between general explanations and events at individual banks, I will argue, is as follows. Many banking activities have profit streams that are fairly stable across different periods.[11] But there are others that generate attractive and steady profits for a number of periods when market conditions are benign, but are inherently risky and thus likely to create a large loss eventually. These behavioural patterns are imprudent in that long-term risks of large losses more than offset a period of profits. Nevertheless, we find that these behaviour patterns occur repeatedly, though often in different guises.

These imprudent behaviour patterns generate profits particularly in periods of steady macroeconomic growth, increasing asset prices, normal upwards-sloping yield curves and high liquidity. (In other words, the conditions that prevailed in the fifteen years before the credit crunch, as explained by the macro and the policy-error camps. Steady economic growth, rising house and asset prices, and low interest rates have kept loan losses low for everyone and have made all types of imprudent behaviour profitable for several years.[12]) They are similarly nearly always behind financial crises. I call the most common of these behaviours the seven deadly sins of imprudent banking.

---

[11] Deposit taking and payment processing come to mind, as do household mortgages that require substantial down payments. For instance, even during the Swedish banking crisis and real estate crash, which we will discuss further in the chapter on Handelsbanken's history, profits and asset quality in household mortgages did not change much.

[12] See Taylor (2009), pp. 31-44, and Haldane (2009) for some empirical evidence that recent years were unusually benign.

1. Asset/Liability Mismatches

Since banks' assets and liabilities are a multiple (often twenty or thirty times) of shareholders' equity, it is important that assets and liabilities react in the same way to changes in the environment, as any divergence has the potential to reduce equity significantly. Nearly all of the assets and liabilities are financial, so the main dimensions in which they should be closely matched are maturity, duration (interest rate sensitivity), and currencies.

While banks are usually involved in some form of maturity transformation there is a risk that, if liabilities have a much shorter maturity, the bank cannot refinance itself and faces a liquidity shortfall. The Irish banking sector, for instance, has financed household mortgages that have a contractual maturity of twenty or more years (though they were usually refinanced or repaid much earlier) to a large extent by commercial paper with a maturity of less than one year. When the credit crunch closed other, longer term, funding sources for them and customers could no longer remortgage, they were left with a massive imbalance. The banks had to roll over large parts of the funding for their loan book every few months, which eventually forced the Irish government to guarantee bank debt to avoid a Northern Rock situation. On top of this maturity mismatch there was a duration mismatch. Mortgages were fixed or base rate linked, while funding was linked to LIBOR (London Interbank Offered Rate), so rising LIBOR spreads reduced mortgage margins significantly.

These liquidity imbalances are by no means new. They featured quite regularly in banking crises in the past – think of Continental Illinois losing USD 10 billion of deposits in spring 1984, or the Japanese banking system in 1998, which was heavily reliant on wholesale funding but had 60% of it in overnight money.[13] The reason these banks cannot roll their funding has often to do with concerns about their solvency – but they get into trouble through liquidity issues regardless of whether these concerns are valid.

It can be very difficult for investors to detect mismatches in asset/liability maturities because banks are obliged to report the maturity structure of their balance sheets only annually and only for the one day on which their financial year ends.[14] That means that banks could be running a fairly substantial liquidity risk, which can bizarrely improve their profit and loss account as it increases net interest income.

Many banks have a structural duration mismatch: they pay more or less variable rates on their customer deposits but lock in much longer rates on their loans. To the extent that usually longer interest rates are higher, this is a source of interest income from taking on interest rate risk. It can, however, go spectacularly wrong if interest rates unexpectedly rise so the bank has to pay more on their deposits without earning more on their loans. In the US Savings and Loans Crisis of the 1980s this was a major factor that caused mass insolvencies when the Federal Reserve System (the Fed) decided to tame inflation by raising interest rates (thrifts had three-quarters of their assets in fixed rate assets while funding was mostly variable).

Duration mismatches, like maturity mismatches, are difficult to spot for investors. They can account for a sizeable share of interest income while having the potential to create big losses. Asset/liability mismatches "work", i.e. are profitable with low volatilities, in the benign macroeconomic environment we discussed. There is ample liquidity, so

---

[13] Bank of International Settlement (2004), p. 62, and Nakaso (2001), p. 36.

[14] Reporting the position for just one day is problematic. Some banks massage their balance sheets for that one reporting date, so it may not reflect the average position over the year.

earning the liquidity premium from maturity mismatches is not very risky. Interest rates are predictable and upward sloping so interest rates on relatively long assets are higher than the rates paid on shorter liabilities. Exchange rates are relatively stable so currency mismatches or carry trades, i.e. borrowing in a currency with low interest rates such as the Yen or Swiss Franc to invest in a currency with higher interest rates, yield steady gains. These mismatches have little to do with banks' franchise operations. But they present a tempting opportunity to boost profits significantly during the good times in a way that is virtually indistinguishable from net interest income in the core or franchise operation.

Although we talk about closing asset/liability mismatches, these should not be limited to items that are recorded on a balance sheet. They should include off-balance positions such as derivatives. The distinction between items on and off a balance sheet is in many cases rather arbitrary and varies massively between accounting standards. The important point is that the overall net position is as closely matched as possible. Running mismatched net positions can generate handsome profits for some time but can also lead to a severe crisis.

2. Supporting Clients' Balance Sheet Mismatches

Financial institutions sometimes have a spotless asset/liability match, but might still face essentially the same problem if their customers do not. Now any change in funding availability, interest rates or currencies can render the borrower unable to service his debt. Should this happen the problem returns to the bank in the guise of credit losses. This is so common and has caused so many banking crises that it is really surprising it has not been stopped long ago.[15]

---

[15] Cf. Minsky (1986), p. 232: 'the existence of a large component of positions financed in a speculative or a Ponzi manner is necessary for financial instability.'

Because banks' accounts reveal next to nothing about the financial situation of their borrowers this, like the first deadly sin, remains invisible even to the most careful reader of banks' financial statements. With Basel II, banks report on the distribution of loans by internal rating categories. This is a step in the right direction but still informs investors only about the bank's opinion of its customers and not about the balance sheet situation of the customers themselves.

This was a major factor in the Latin American markets crisis of the early 1980s. Mexico, Brazil, Argentina and others could no longer service debt that was denominated in USD and had rapidly rising interest rates. It played a similar role in the Swedish/Scandinavian banking crisis of the early 1990s, where many corporate borrowers avoided high interest rates in their own currencies by borrowing in Deutschmarks. When local currencies, in which most of their income was denominated, depreciated against the Deutschmark while interest rates shot up, they could not service their debt. The same problem occurred in the Asian crisis later that decade, where debt denominated in foreign currencies ballooned in local currency terms as local currencies depreciated.

And today? Indian companies that borrow in Swiss francs have as little income or assets in that currency as Hungarian households that have a mortgage in Swiss francs or yen.

A very similar phenomenon is teaser rates, i.e. loans that have no or low interest payments for a certain period before they reset to a higher level of interest payments. This is a widespread phenomenon in the US mortgage market and in consumer lending such as credit cards or auto loans (those "0% for 24 months" offers). Of course this is never matched by a corresponding increase in the borrower's income, which leads us to the third deadly sin.

3. Lending to Over-Indebted Customers

A related but slightly different imprudent stance is to lend to customers who cannot afford the loan. It is related to the previous sin because accepting customer mismatches is often one way of making a loan appear more affordable than it really is. Where customers borrow in foreign currencies the reason is often that interest rates are lower so the instalments on the loan are more affordable. But there are many more ways to lend to customers who should not borrow.

Customers should be able to finance their lifestyle (individuals) or operations (companies) from regular income, and any additional loan they take up should be serviced with any extra free income. Although this is common sense it is frequently ignored. A large proportion of subprime customers could not afford to buy a home and could not service the mortgage from their income, hence the shenanigans to make the deals seem better than they were, for instance by mortgages that did not amortise.

Another example is using your home as a cash machine by taking up a mortgage to maintain unsustainable consumption levels (related to the so-called Duesenberry effect) which is widespread in several Eastern European countries.[16] Private equity companies have often loaded up the companies they have bought with so much debt at the peak of the economic cycle that even these very good times would have had to improve further to allow the companies to repay their loans. Canadian department store magnate Robert Campeau could bid for

---

[16] The orthodox view in economics is that individuals rationally adjust their consumption to future expected earnings. James Duesenberry broke with this view (as had earlier economists such as Thorstein Veblen) and went back to a more sociological explanation. According to him, consumption levels were set relative to one's own past consumption and to what others are consuming ("keeping up with the Joneses"). If income drops to a permanently lower level, the orthodox expectation is that people will spend less while the Duesenberry effect would lead us to expect increasing indebtedness to maintain consumption.

Bloomingdale's in 1988 with less than 2% in his own equity. Operating cash flows were insufficient to service the mountain of debt incurred in the acquisition.[17]

As mentioned for the previous deadly sin, since banks' financial statements include virtually no information about the finances of their borrowers, lending to those who cannot afford it does not show up in banks' accounts.

Apart from the folly of lending to those who may not be able to repay their loan, the trouble with high leverage is that it allows problems to spread through the system rapidly when each element of the chain is too weakly capitalised to withstand any shock.

4. Investing in Non-Core Assets

Should a US investment bank be the biggest owner of Japanese golf courses? Should European postal savings banks hold bundles of American mortgages to subprime clients? Or large portfolios of international real estate? A Swedish bank hold mortgages on Lehman property? The fourth deadly sin is so obvious that it does not need further elaboration.

When banks own assets that have absolutely nothing to do with their real business, simply because they seem low risk and yield a juicy return, more often than not it ends in tears. Perhaps it all sounds so attractive simply because it is not your expertise. Why else would the previous owner want to sell them?

Nevertheless, banks' balance sheets in the US and in Europe have shifted markedly in this direction. According to data by the US Federal

---

[17] Chancellor (1999), p. 277.

Deposit Insurance Corporation in 1971, government (guaranteed) debt accounted for 98% of the fixed income security holdings of US commercial banks. In 2007 this had fallen to 69% while nearly one-third of the holdings were now structured credit instruments and corporate bonds. These are unsuitable as a liquidity buffer (in times of stress, i.e. when the buffer is needed, only treasuries tend to trade actively). Their apparent attraction is that they pay spreads that are higher, not lower, than bank's own funding costs, allowing banks to turn a liquidity portfolio in their treasury operations from loss making to profit making.

> " When banks own assets that have absolutely nothing to do with their real business, more often than not it ends in tears. "

Needless to say, when credit spreads widened in 2007/08, these instruments were useless as a liquidity holding and accrued losses several times higher than the cumulative profit made on them.

Many non-core financial assets on banks' balance sheets are shock amplifiers. In good times their value increases, which gives banks more capital to create new loans which in turn support the value of their non-core financial assets. In bad times, however, this process goes in reverse. Japanese banks in the 1990s were faced with capital erosion as the value of the cross-shareholdings fell. In the current financial crisis structured credit plays a similar role.

We will discuss Handelsbanken's different approach in the chapter on their risk management philosophy. It distinguishes between risks the bank willingly accepts as it can manage them better than anyone else (the credit risk of their customers) and all other risks which are minimised even at the cost of losing significant income.

5. Dealing with the Non-Bank Financial System

What is just outside the official banking system has an uncanny ability to cause systemic instability. Non-bank finance companies at least triggered the banking crises in Sweden (Nyckeln) and Japan (first credit cooperatives, then *jusen* or housing loan corporations, later securities houses) in the 1990s. The collapse of Long-Term Capital Management (LTCM), a large hedge fund, in the wake of the 1998 Russian crisis was seen as a threat to the entire financial system.

Conduits, SIVs (structured investment vehicles) and other off-balance sheet vehicles that were meant to be separate from the banks starting them came to haunt their creators in 2007 and 2008. *Plus ça change*: the conduit and SIV situation is very similar to the US REIT (real estate investment trust) crisis in 1983/4 and illustrates why the non-bank financial system poses such high risks. It accumulates risks from indulging in other deadly sins such as investing in risky long assets (real estate developments in the case of the REITs, structured credit instruments in the case of conduits/SIVs) financed with short liabilities (commercial paper then, asset backed commercial paper now). When funding on the open market dries up, these off-balance sheet vehicles fall back on the official banking system's liquidity back-up lines. Official banks thereby *de facto* assume problem assets of the shadow banking system on their own balance sheet.

Often the assets of the official and the shadow banking system are similar. That implies banks assume problem assets from the shadow banking system at the worst possible time, since a deterioration of their own assets has already weakened their balance sheets.

The unofficial banking system is part of the rest of the financial system. It serves as an unregulated source of credit expansion (e.g. collateralised loan obligations (CLOs), which fund over half of leveraged loans). The IMF estimates that it is huge, accounting for $10 trillion assets in 2007 in the US alone, equal in size to the official banking system. The shadow banking system is rather opaque, insufficiently supervised (which often also means that there are no tools to bail out its members) and has a very concentrated risk profile with often weak, myopic risk management capabilities.[18] Similarly, imprudent behaviour is often to be found after periods of financial deregulation when institutions with insufficient experience or structures enjoy strong new growth.

6. Münchhausen Markets: Emerging Markets and Real Estate

The legendary Baron Münchhausen fell into a swamp and gloriously pulled himself out by his own bootstraps. Similarly, some banking markets appear attractive only because banks make them so. But bankers have as little faith in their capacity to engineer a positive macroeconomic situation as they would have in Münchhausen's feat; so they believe that the positive fundamentals must have been there before them. No more is needed to start a self-reinforcing cycle that goes through boom and bust.

Two sectors that have played a major part in most banking crises are real estate lending and emerging markets banking. Unlike the first five deadly sins they are not wrong in themselves: there are prudent, stable ways of banking with both areas, some of which we will discuss for Handelsbanken specifically. Yet, more often than not, real estate lending and emerging markets banking lead to a crisis: it is surprising that banks quickly forget how often these areas have brought them into severe

---

[18] 'Market discipline (coupled with weakened prudential regulation) was apparently ineffective in constraining risk-taking outside the banking sector', IMF (February 2009), p. 9.

trouble. The basic problem is that they are cyclical because they are for some time self-reinforcing. In real estate, credit expansion leads to increased demand for a fixed supply of real estate so asset price increases. With rising asset prices even problem cases rarely lead to a loss because selling the collateral at a higher price more than covers the loan. Lending standards are relaxed since risks appear negligible, further fuelling credit expansion and taking care of problem cases since it is easy to refinance. This is the narrative gleaned from senior loan officer surveys in the US and Europe.[19]

Similar mechanisms are often at work in emerging markets. As long as there is enough risk appetite to transfer funds on a large scale to emerging markets, these funds lead to strong economic growth. How can a country such as Ukraine not grow its economy very strongly during a period where lending increases by more than 50% per year from 2004 to 2008? In these years when banks are happy to lend to emerging markets everything looks benign: banks make large profits, asset quality is good, the country is growing strongly. This means more demand for banking products, even more growth and profits etc, so shareholders or regulators looking at numbers will find absolutely nothing to be unhappy about.[20] It takes a fool not to make money for a consecutive number of years in the real estate and emerging markets upswing.[21]

---

[19] Also see Taylor (2008) for empirical data on the relationship of house prices and defaults.

[20] As Minsky puts it: 'good times induce balance-sheet adventuring. The process by which speculative finance increases, as a proportion of the total financing of business, leads to higher asset prices and to increased investment. This leads to an improvement in employment, output, and business profits, which in turn proves to businessmen and bankers that experimenting with speculative finance was correct.' (Minsky 1986, p. 42).

[21] A fate that Handelsbanken in its early days did not avoid. Via a closely related company, Svenska Emissionsaktiebolaget, Handelsbanken started speculating on international trade connections with Russia, Latin America and others around WWI. 'A notable lightheartedness was evident in the handling of some of these affairs. The profits were dazzling at first, but when they dried up the ensuing loss was a very heavy one' (Hildebrand 1971, p. 29).

Unsurprisingly, this whole self-reinforcing cycle can just as easily go into reverse. The moment international banks pull back there is a high likelihood that economic growth will come to an abrupt halt and asset quality will deteriorate sharply.

Barings' first brush with bankruptcy in 1890 came from its dealing in loans to Argentina. Citi's last encounter with insolvency is only a quarter of a century old: the emerging markets debt crisis meant that Citicorp faced large burdens of bad debt from lending to developing countries that later defaulted.[22]

The IMF database of banking crises (Laeven/Valencia 2008) is full of systemic bank failures in emerging markets. Some of them caused significant losses also for the banking system in the developed world (the already mentioned Latin American debt crisis in the 1980s, the Asian crisis 1997, the Russian crisis 1998, and the Argentina crisis 2001).

> **Markets that everyone else finds unattractive can bizarrely be safer environments because they lack the self-reinforcing boom and bust cycle.**

Today there are real concerns about the implications that banking in Eastern Europe would have on Western European banks. Handelsbanken's credit risk officer once quipped that lending in some Eastern European countries was 'the closest in Europe to subprime lending'; banks were offering loans to inexperienced borrowers in foreign currencies.

---

[22] Citicorp's chairman Walter Wriston is still famous for his quote, 'countries don't go bust'. Well, until they did, partly because they had borrowed in foreign currencies which they could not print – see deadly sin number two.

Real estate or emerging markets banking becomes problematic only because the activity of banks creates what everybody believes to be the underlying fundamentals. The reason is that credit and credit growth are a more important driver for the development of housing and emerging markets than for many others. More lending leads to growth and asset price increases while risks remain low. Attributing these "fundamentals" to secular trends attracts more bankers keen to participate, so the cycle gets reinforced. But emerging markets and real estate are relatively safe only where just a few banks operate and the resulting credit expansion is moderate.

Markets that everyone else finds unattractive or too risky can thus bizarrely be safer environments because they lack the self-reinforcing boom and bust cycle.

7. The Continuity of the Past to the Future

It is intuitively very plausible that recent trends will continue in the future and that patterns of relationship that have been observed will remain. It is also very dangerous and potentially misleading if it is true that the seven deadly sins can lead to a string of profitable years before ending in crisis.

Expecting the future to be a continuation of the past is problematic on several levels. Developing a bank's strategy and thinking about which markets to participate in usually relies on an analysis of the profitability and growth trends of the different market segments. Prioritising those markets with strong growth and profitability in the past, on the expectation that these will continue, can lead a bank to enter a market at its peak. We will discuss this fallacy further when we compare the Handelsbanken approach to strategy with the portfolio approach which most other banks follow – and which is prone to this error.

For risk management, especially in the trading book, it can be fatal. There are obvious possibilities that have no precedent. It may be true that there has been no prolonged drop in US house prices in history but this would not lead any sensible person to conclude that it cannot happen in the future. Yet this is what often happens in risk management and capital planning. Northern Rock's scenario planning did not include a long shut-down of wholesale funding markets. Shiller (2008, p. 52) recalls a debate in 2006 (in the preceding decade house prices had increased by 85%) with the chief economist of Freddie Mac in which the latter defended the fact that Freddie's worst stress test was for a 13.4% fall in house prices arguing that a bigger drop had not occurred since the Great Depression. I am sure that his statistical analysis is correct but would it not strike you as showing a lack of imagination when the worst situation a big mortgage player can think of is that prices are still up 60% from ten years ago?

It has become rather fashionable since the publication of Taleb's book to qualify recent events as "black swan events". Black swan events may be more frequent in finance than most people in finance realise. But calling everything untoward a black swan lets most practitioners off the hook too easily – which is perhaps why the theory has been endorsed so enthusiastically.

Annual reports explicitly or implicitly describe the credit crunch as unprecedented and beyond anybody's wildest imagination, implying that no management should be held responsible for the fallout. In reality, financial crises have been too frequent to make this argument plausible. The financial services industry likes to make it sound as though we are witnessing the impossible.

David Viniar, the Chief Financial Officer of Goldman Sachs, said in August 2007 that the firm's hedge funds 'were seeing things that were 25-standard deviation moves, several days in a row,' implying that things were happening time and again that should be very unlikely to happen even once in a lifetime.

In reality, the market movements of August 2007, though certainly large, did not stun people in the way September 11 did, since many had seen similar events before (e.g. in 1987).[23] The models were simply wrong, grossly underestimating the

> **" Calling everything untoward a black swan lets most practitioners off the hook too easily. "**

probability of scenarios that were intuitively at least conceivable if not plausible.

What is to blame is the reliance on historical data for risk modelling. By definition it puts very low probabilities on events that we can think of which are perfectly conceivable, but have not happened yet. As these models are also used to quantify the amount of capital a bank needs to hold, the banks allocate too little capital to activities with large downside risks. The use of these models are thus responsible for the fact that banks engage in such activities – they do not penalise imprudent activities sufficiently versus prudent ones. If these scenarios materialise, the bank as a whole is likely to find itself undercapitalised. We will come back to this point in discussing Handelsbanken's risk management approach and what the Handelsbanken model implies for bank regulation.

---

[23] But then defenders of their models already declared the 1987 stock market crash an impossibility: see Chancellor (1999), p. 282.

The Temptations of the Seven Deadly Sins

The seven deadly sins are frequently recurring microeconomic behaviour patterns that can cause financial crises. Unlike other efforts to classify elements of financial crises they are not just environmental factors that support crises, nor are they a taxonomy of how crises develop. What are the reasons that banks still engage in the seven deadly sins? There are several common ones.

Riding the (risky) waves

One is the belief that one can ride the trend even if one knows that it will end in despair. Perhaps the best evidence is the well-known quote by former Citi CEO Charles Prince: 'as long as the music is playing, you've got to get up and dance. We're still dancing.'[24]

Peer pressure

Peer pressure is another reason why banks engaged in imprudent practices. For lending to households in Eastern Europe in euros, Swiss francs or yen, the epitome of the second deadly sin, I have heard from three different CEOs of major banks in the region that they admit it should not be done. They added that they preferred it to be banned by the regulator – but that they had to do it if they did not want to lose market share since everybody else did it. The Bank of England laconically states that its 'market intelligence suggested this "keeping up with the Joneses" was a potent force within financial firms during the upswing.'[25] Kindleberger describes this phenomenon when he says that

---

[24] Nothing new to the banker who in 1720 subscribed to £500 of South Sea stock since 'when the rest of the world are mad, we must imitate them in some measure' (quoted after Kindleberger 2000, p. 26).

[25] Haldane (2009), p. 6.

he has often got a nervous laugh from the audience when he stated that 'there is nothing so disturbing to one's well-being and judgement as to see a friend get rich'.[26]

Vainglorious bankers

A third reason has to do with managerial vanity, or in the words of Mervyn King: 'it is not easy to persuade people, especially those who are earning vast sums as a result, that what looks successful in the short run is actually highly risky in the long run [...] and individuals are reluctant to accept that success may not be the result of superior wisdom, which should naturally be reflected in compensation, but the short-run outcome of a risky strategy.'[27]

When we discuss how Handelsbanken's model is more resistant to the seven deadly sins we shall come back to these first three reasons in the context of Handelsbanken's culture and incentive system.

Undifferentiated financial statements

There is another very simple reason why the seven deadly sins are still abundant, namely that in the financial statements of banks and financial institutions prudent and imprudent profits look alike. In other industries

---

[26] Kindleberger (2000), p. 15. The peer pressure among banks has always reminded me of the anecdote by Oscar Wilde: 'the devil was once crossing the Libyan desert, and he came upon a spot where a number of small fiends were tormenting a holy hermit. The sainted man easily shook off their evil suggestions. The devil watched their failure, and then he stepped forward to give them a lesson. "What you do is too crude," he said. "Permit me for one moment." With that he whispered to the holy man, "Your brother has just been made Bishop of Alexandria." A scowl of malignant jealousy at once clouded the serene face of the hermit. "That," said the devil to his imps, "is the sort of thing which I should recommend".' (quoted by Arthur Conan Doyle in his autobiography *Memories and Adventures*, p. 66).

[27] Speech on March 17th, 2009.

speculative activity is reported separately so investors can differentiate core operations from pure gambling. The money Porsche made from selling cars is clearly distinguishable in its accounts (as "operating performance") from money it made from dealing in shares and options of Volkswagen.[28]

For financial institutions, on the other hand, the income statement does not distinguish the two: the balance sheet gives little or no information about the speculative risk incurred. For instance, income attributable to asset and liability mismatches – the first of the seven deadly sins – is reported as net interest income just like customer related income. On the balance sheet, loans to customers that are mismatched or over-indebted are indistinguishable from others since they are all aggregated into one line: "customer loans".

Similarly, risky non-core assets such as structured credit instruments are often not distinguished from risk-free instruments. This lack of distinction between prudent and imprudent profits explains why banks voluntarily engage in the seven deadly sins.[29] Often banks facing pressure in their core operations are tempted to enter imprudent activities to offset an underlying decline in profits, and the speculative results are amalgamated with the underlying performance into a reported profit figure.

---

[28] Porsche, a small but profitable luxury carmaker, followed a cunning strategy in taking over the much larger car producer Volkswagen. In the process Porsche bought options to buy Volkswagen shares, which appreciated in value as Volkswagen's share price rose. In the first six months of its 2008/09 business year Porsche made EUR 6.8 billion from Volkswagen options and EUR 0.5 billion from selling cars. From their income statement it is clear what the contribution of financial speculation is – which for banks is nearly impossible to quantify from the outside.

[29] Chancellor (1999) blames misleading accounting, i.e. recording profits from dealing in own shares, for earlier crises: 'these arrangements were as confusing to most contemporaries as they appear to the modern reader [...] this basic accounting error contributed greatly to the blowing up of the Mississippi and South Sea bubbles' (ibid., p. 62).

Problems Resisting the Sins

What is rather concerning about the seven deadly sins is that although they are responsible for most episodes of financial instability, there is no external pressure for institutions to stay well clear of them. Shareholders are more than happy to go along while things go well and indulging in one or more of the seven deadly sins is very profitable.

Nor do regulators think in these categories. Some of the seven deadly sins are outside their field of vision altogether (for instance, the second sin of pushing balance sheet mismatches to customers), or regulators are at best colour blind to others (for instance, a rather rudimentary differentiation between loans to creditworthy and over-indebted customers). Focusing on (capital) ratios is a form of sin number seven and simply not meaningful if the nature of the underlying business implies that the ratios could change rather quickly.[30] Unsurprisingly, in a recent report the IMF found that the ratios regulators routinely use did not identify the institutions that ran into trouble. On the contrary: those banks that subsequently required government support had looked substantially stronger with regard to capitalisation and asset quality![31]

Ratios for prudent banking activities are relatively stable while those for activities that fall under the seven deadly sins can behave in very non-linear ways and change very quickly. The solidity of a bank is not about its current shape but about the shape it would be in under a number of stress scenarios. This implies that capital requirements for prudent and imprudent activities should be different. Asking for higher

---

[30] The central banker in charge of dealing with the Japanese banking crisis acknowledges this problem: 'even if a bank examiner [from] the [Central] Bank suspected [the] over-concentration of credit risk of a bank in the real estate sector, it could have been practically difficult for the [C]entral [B]ank to intervene as long as the loans were performing and the bank did not suffer losses' (Nakaso 2001, p.18).

[31] IMF (April 2009), chapter three "Detecting Systemic Risks".

capital requirements across the board seems an inefficient way to deal with the issue that regulators fail to distinguish between prudent and imprudent activities.

To borrow from Harold Macmillan, we had never had it so good – all these imprudent strategies brought in steadily growing profits, year after year. And suddenly they all turned sour. This partly explains the cognitive disconnect between the banking industry and the general public. For the public hearing about stupendous losses, it is clear that managers of these institutions must have made spectacular errors of judgement or even behaved criminally. These managers, on the other hand, do not see what they have done differently from 2007 onwards compared to the preceding decade where they were applauded (and rewarded) as heroes and geniuses. As a result, they see themselves as victims of a radical, "black swan", change in the environment.

Handelsbanken looked wrong-footed when it did not participate in the seven deadly sins, but is in an enviable position today. It is one of the few large-scale examples of truly prudent banking. To see all types of institutions first succumb, then suffer from, the seven deadly sins shows that remaining prudent is very difficult when few others are. Part II is dedicated to a detailed description of Handelsbanken's model and why they avoided so many pitfalls when most of their peers were making large profits from them. Many other financial institutions were attracted by the siren songs of the seven deadly sins and found their ruin. Ulysses avoided the sirens by putting wax in the ears of his crew and being tied to the mast of his ship. What were the precautions that Handelsbanken took in order not to succumb?

Part II

The Handelsbanken Way of Banking

4

History

S venska Handelsbanken was founded, under the name of Stockholms Handelsbank, in 1871 by a group of directors of Wallenberg's Stockholms Enskilda Bank who had left after conflict with the strong willed managing director. It was the bank of Stockholm's merchants, who both owned the shares and used its services. Despite having only a handful of staff it had relationships with other banks in Hamburg, Altona, London, and Paris. The bank remained relatively small for 22 years until Louis Fraenckel, a banker of German extraction, became managing director in 1893 and pushed the bank to grow rapidly.

Interestingly, Fraenckel held views that would not sound alien to the current management. For instance he had an international outlook (sending staff to Australia and South Africa). Also, he maintained that a bank should not lend to doubtful borrowers on the basis of someone's guarantee, but rather evaluate the borrower in his own right and lend on this basis alone. There are also his fierce protection of clients' confidentiality and a tendency to build capital reserves.

In the first two decades of the new century, Handelsbanken took part very actively in the banking mergers in Sweden that transformed a number of essentially local banks into a few truly country-wide institutions, one of which has carried, since 1919, the name Svenska Handelsbanken.

While the bank had grown rapidly up to 1914, it still had only seven branches, but through four major mergers between 1914 and 1919 it became the largest Swedish bank, with nearly 300 branch offices nationwide. The bank for many decades continued to acquire smaller regional banks in Sweden and then across Scandinavia.

Handelsbanken did not escape the financial crises of the 1920s and 1930s. It had to take over de facto ownership of a number of its borrowers and restructure them. Parts of the portfolio were listed as a separate company, Industrivärden, in 1945. Today this fund is one of the main shareholders in Handelsbanken, with approximately 10% ownership.

Decentralisation

The early history of the bank is not markedly different from that of other Swedish or European banks. So we should jump to 1970, when Jan Wallander became chief executive and laid down, 99 years after the bank's foundation, the key principles that interest us in this book.

Wallander describes the bank he found, when he was appointed chief executive with a rescue mission, as follows. Under the influence of US management methods the bank had adopted a functional, centralised organisation. It held the belief that a credit decision became more informed the higher up in the organisation it was taken and the more people were involved. This meant that a credit decision took on average two months before the customer got a yes or no. In 1968 over 2400 loan applications had to be decided by the management board or the board of directors.[32]

Wallander transformed Handelsbanken into the more risk-averse and decentralised organisation that I will describe in the following chapters. This attitude allowed the bank to survive the Swedish banking crisis in the early 1990s relatively unscathed.

---

[32] Wallander (2004), pp. 33-37

Crisis Survival

Following deregulation in the mid-1980s, Sweden had experienced a massive lending boom. Loans to the private sector increased from 85% of GDP in 1985 to 135% five years later. This led to strong increases in real estate prices, which grew by 125% over the same period. Half of all corporate loans were in foreign currencies such as the Deutschmark. This was because the Swedish crown was anchored to the Deutschmark in the ERM while having much higher interest rates as domestic inflation was high. This system was very fragile on a micro and macro level, and it needed only a small external trigger to bring it down: the Riksbank was forced to increase interest rates as the Bundesbank raised interest rates in the wake of German reunification. In addition, the ERM collapsed in November 1992 with the Swedish crown devaluing against the Deutschmark. Sharply falling house prices since 1991, high interest rates and a debt burden that had increased markedly as a result of the devaluation meant that many customers could not pay their loans and banks found themselves faced with substantial bad loans. These were initially concentrated in the real estate sector and in loans to finance companies that had often made real estate loans themselves. But as the economy contracted by 6% and industrial output fell by 17% over three years, most other sectors experienced substantial bankruptcies, too.[33]

---

[33] For more information on the Swedish banking crisis see Lindgren/Wallander/Sjöberg (1994); Martin Andersson and Staffan Viotti: "Managing and Preventing Financial Crises – Lessons from the Swedish Experience", *Riksbank Quarterly Review* 1, 1999, pp. 71-89; "Knut Sandal: The Nordic banking crises in the early 1990s–resolution methods and fiscal costs", in: The Norwegian Banking Crisis, Norges Bank Occasional Papers 33, 2004, p. 77-115; O. Emre Ergungor: "On the Resolution of Financial Crises: The Swedish Experience", Federal Reserve Bank of Cleveland Policy Discussion Paper 21, 2007; Peter Englund: "The Swedish Banking Crisis – Roots and Consequences", in: *Oxford Review of Economic Policy* 15, 1999, pp. 80-97.

While all other large banks were nationalised or needed to apply for state support to balance massive loan losses, Handelsbanken made only an insignificant loss in the worst year of the crisis, 1992: a -3% return on equity compared to -55% for the entire banking sector. Profits before loan losses even increased 20%.

In the deep recession the bank did not wholly avoid difficulties in areas which caused its peers massive problems. In 1992 the loan loss ratio for loans to construction and property companies was 7.5%, for loans to finance companies 10.5% and for leveraged acquisition loans 26.2%. Still, these sectors were smaller in Handelsbanken's loan book than the market average. More importantly, the bank had picked better borrowers across sectors: for the overall loan book the loss ratio was only 2.5%, less than half the banking sector average of 5.4% and well below the 8% and 19% for the two large banks that had to be nationalised. Its market share of total Swedish loans had been 25% in 1990 but it suffered only 9% of all loan losses from 1990-93.

Handelsbanken did not set up its own "bad bank" but it transferred repossessed real estate – collateral which the bank had to take over from defaulted borrowers – to a new subsidiary called Näckebro. Handelsbanken's shares in Näckebro were subsequently distributed to Handelsbanken's shareholders.

Crisis Triumph

Overall, the bank traded through the crisis well and at the end found itself in a much stronger position, with significantly higher market shares.

It learnt its lessons in risk management. For instance, the bank stopped lending where it did not control the underwriting, thereby ruling out loans to finance companies. Handelsbanken also focused even more closely on the cash flow situation of borrowers (can they afford the loan? are they running unsuitable mismatches?) and put even less trust on the value of collateral. In 1996, operating profits were nearly 50% higher than in the pre-crisis record year 1990, while for the overall banking sector they remained more or less flat.[34]

Handelsbanken

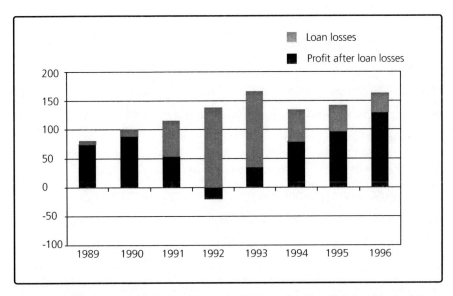

Figure 2.1: Operating profit development during the Swedish banking crisis – Handelsbanken [1990=100]

---

[34] Operating profit, i.e. before loan losses, is the better metric to compare pre and post crisis profitability. Handelsbanken's peers started experiencing higher loan losses already in 1990 (cont.)

Swedish banking system overall

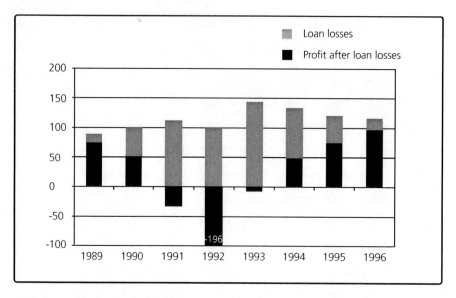

Figure 2.2: Operating profit development during the Swedish banking crisis – banking system overall [1990=100]

In a sector that is plagued by profit distributions like those of the seven deadly sins, i.e. many years of high profits, then a large loss, Handelsbanken appear to do the opposite: years of more pedestrian profits but then a significant, permanent step up when everybody else is getting into trouble.

There have been hundreds of papers on the Swedish banking crisis and its resolution in macroeconomic terms. Yet, strangely enough, nobody ever seems to have wondered why one fairly large bank avoided large losses, did not need state support and came out of the crisis much stronger.

---

and benefited in the mid-1990s from larger releases from loan loss provisions. In other words, their profits after loan losses are depressed in 1990 and inflated in the mid-1990s. I am grateful to Jonas Ehrnst from Statistiska centralbyrån for some of the underlying data.

Swedish Context

The bank's goal is to earn a higher return on equity than the average of its peer group, and 2008 was the 36th consecutive year in which this goal was achieved.

Banking in Sweden today is not much different from most other Western countries. Its regulatory system resembles that of the UK. The country has four large banks – Swedbank, a merger of savings banks and still with a main focus on banking with individuals and small companies; SEB, the bank partly owned by the influential Wallenberg family and today the foremost corporate and merchant bank although also with a strong presence among more affluent individual clients; Nordea, the result of cross-country mergers of banks in Scandinavia and today the largest Scandinavian bank (it incorporates Nordbanken and Gotabanken, the two Swedish banks that had to be nationalised during the crisis); and Svenska Handelsbanken.

In addition, some foreign banks such as Danske Bank of Denmark have operations with sizeable branch networks in Sweden. Swedbank and Handelsbanken are the largest banks in terms of branch networks (Handelsbanken edged ahead slightly at the end of 2008 and now leads the country with 461 branches across Sweden) and have about one quarter of the market share each in household mortgages.

Traditionally, Handelsbanken has had, on the retail banking side, older and more affluent customers and, on the corporate banking side, a stronger presence in small and medium enterprises. Mass market customers are usually served more by Swedbank and Nordea, while large corporates tend to have stronger relationships with SEB. But, again, given the large position of all four banks in Sweden these are nuances.

Handelsbanken offers its customers a full range of banking products. At its core are branch operations in Sweden, the other Scandinavian countries, the UK and, to a smaller extent, some other European countries. Its capital markets division includes all investment banking services that customers need. In advisory, bond and equity underwriting, syndicated lending and offering clients equities, debt and commodities trading Handelsbanken is one of the biggest players in Scandinavia. Handelsbanken's asset management division provides mutual funds and is a large player in exchange traded funds in Scandinavia. The division also includes a life insurance company, Liv.

So Handelsbanken is certainly not a niche player. It serves most types of customer, offering them the full range of banking products.

During the current financial crisis Handelsbanken has practised "business as usual" to a greater extent than other banks. It has been able to fund itself continuously in the wholesale market with long maturity debt in spite of being the only large Nordic bank that does not make use of government guarantees. Since it is seen as the safest bank, Handelsbanken takes in large amounts of customer and institutional deposits without competing on price. It also keeps lending to its customers as before. As most competitors have withdrawn or reduced their lending, Handelsbanken is gaining new customers at a fast pace and is benefiting from higher spreads on new loans. Loan losses are increasing, as is to be expected in a global recession, but at a more moderate pace than for its peers. This remarkable performance lies behind the equally remarkable development of its share price. (See performance table in Figure 3).

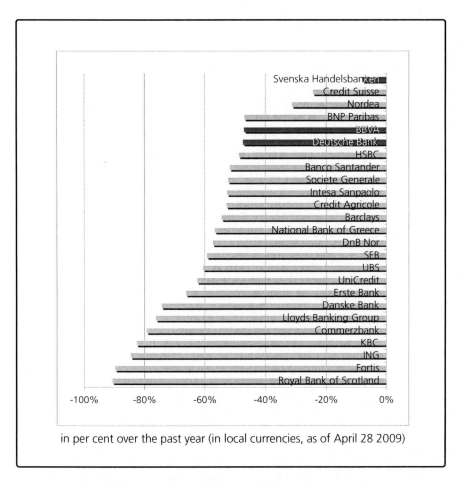

in per cent over the past year (in local currencies, as of April 28 2009)

Figure 3: Share price performance of the largest European banks – only the three banks shaded in dark did not have to get government support or raise capital

5

Strategy and Business Focus

Decentralisation, a Fundamentally Simple Model

'The branch is the Bank' is the summary of Handelsbanken's strategy. When I first heard it my impression was that it was trivial, not saying anything, pure marketing. I have since come to see that it is not. The bank is dead serious in implementing this philosophy.

The idea behind it is that a customer really has a relationship with his bank branch and the people at that branch (every customer at Handelsbanken has one relationship manager, unlike most other banks at which smaller customers hardly ever do). Given that the branch also knows the customer better than anyone else in the bank, the bank believes that the branch should be given wide-ranging freedom on how best to serve the customer. As a consequence, Handelsbanken delegates authority to the branch manager where other banks decide centrally.[35]

---

[35] The following descriptions in Niall Ferguson's *The Pity of War* (1998) reminded me of the different approaches of where to locate organisational authority. Ferguson analyses the reasons for the relatively lower effectiveness of the British military during World War I: 'The trouble was [...] that the entire culture of the British regular army militated against effective improvisation. The command structure was based on obedience to superiors and suspicion of subordinates; men could still advance according to their connections; and commanders could still be "unstuck" by personal quarrels' (ibid., p. 305). To me this seems a fairly accurate description of many banks I know (interestingly, Ferguson himself makes the comparison with private organisations and their idea of "line management"). The German army, according to Ferguson, was organised fundamentally differently, acknowledging the unpredictable complexities of individual situations and accordingly devolving decision making and initiative to the lower ranks close to the situation.

Pricing

Pricing is set by the branch. It can offer each customer a different rate for deposits or for loans. It can even offer the customer a price at which the bank does not make much money, if the staff think this is the right thing to do to enter a long-term relationship. In practice this means that the bank suggests a price for many services which the branch can then keep or vary as it sees fit. Customer pricing is thus not a tool that the bank headquarters uses to manage its business. Other banks would, for instance, offer a bank-wide campaign for a deposit account that pays a good interest rate to customers if the bank wants to grow its deposit base. Handelsbanken has neither campaigns nor bank-wide pricing, and it does not try to influence branch behaviour tactically.

Marketing

Marketing is also done predominantly at branch level (there are some exceptions, for internet savings or new product launches). The bank has hardly any central marketing – which is perhaps why their visibility is relatively low. You will hardly ever see a full page ad by this bank in the national media. It is the responsibility of the branch manager to decide how much to spend on marketing and how. In practice this often means that the bank spends much less than its peers and does mostly local sponsoring. Similarly, the branch manager has discretion over all direct costs so she or he can decide how many people to hire at the branch and how much their salaries should be (though nobody gets a bonus – see below, "Culture and Incentives").

Customer segmentation

Customer segmentation is another area left completely to the discretion of the branch. Bank customers may not be aware that most banks spend an inordinate amount of time thinking about how to segment their customers into subgroups that will then get a differentiated level of service, different product offers and prices. A bank could, for instance, decide that companies with more than fifty employees that are still managed by the owner and have no separate, full-time finance director are a customer segment of itself. The bank would then train relationship managers for this specific group, decide how many of these customers a relationship manager can be expected to serve, how many times per year these customers should be visited, whether the relationship manager should also look after the private finances of the company owner or leave this to a colleague, etc.

At Handelsbanken, the philosophy is that the last person to know the answer to all these questions is the Stockholm head office – further, that all these companies are probably different in some other important ways. As a consequence, the segmentation is left entirely to the branches. The bank's computer system allows the branch manager to create segments of his customers as he sees fit, but it is not mandatory to use this feature. So the customer service model for two similar clients in adjacent towns can be very different.

Localism

To avoid conflicts between branches, each branch can serve customers only from its own region. The bank charmingly calls this the 'church tower principle', as though a branch can only serve customers it can see from a little tower on its branch. There are literally maps with demarcation lines to show which branch is responsible for which territory. This rule is also to ensure that branches know their borrowers well.

Admin/back office

Administration and back office work is – yes, you guessed it – still done at the branch level. While IT and payments are processed centrally (one area where the branches have to go with a central choice), most other processes are completed at the branch level. This means the branch knows the status of all customer transactions: they can make last minute changes or tell a customer immediately if his mortgage has been approved or if a payment has been executed. This would not be so remarkable were it not for the fact that all other large banks I know have centralised back office activities as much as possible, in order to save costs. They may have achieved this goal, but at the cost of less flexibility and less knowledge where things stand, both of which reduce the quality of customer service.

Branch banking in the internet age

The primacy of the branch is so deeply ingrained in the bank's culture that the emergence of internet banking was seen as a threat. If a customer did his or her business on the internet, what relationship would be left with the branch? Handelsbanken's solution is unique in the banking industry and charmingly quaint: each branch got its own website. To be sure, the technology platform in the background is identical; but customers see their local branch, even in cyberspace. If I go to the bank's main internet page I am automatically redirected to the website of my local branch, where I can see photos and contact details of my branch staff. Looking at my account details or making a payment online is thus still somehow done with my branch. The branch can also change the design and functionality of the website. Like marketing, internet banking has become a decentralised and individual tool for each branch.

Credit decisions – decentralised but closely monitored

Perhaps most remarkable is the responsibility of the branches for loan decisions. Not surprisingly, large loans cannot be approved by the branch alone but must be endorsed by the next layer of organisational hierarchy, the regional bank, and very large loans by the central credit organisation or even the board in Stockholm. But no loan gets approved if the local branch officer does not support it. That means that even a loan over several billion Swedish crowns to one of the largest Swedish companies does not happen if the branch manager responsible for that customer is not fully in favour. Pär Boman, the chief executive of the bank since 2006, told me that Handelsbanken looked at problem cases in the past and found that a suspiciously large number of loans that subsequently ran into trouble had in the past been approved by the centre, particularly by some extraordinary board credit committees. As a result, they now stick to the regular process which leaves responsibility first and foremost with the branch.

In this decentralised setting, there is, however, no departure from the bank's credit policy. This is binding for all branches and has not changed much over the past decades. Handelsbanken's current credit risk officer confirmed in a conversation with me that banks in Sweden that subsequently went bankrupt had a high share – up to half of the loan book – decided by their boards. With large numbers of such decisions to be taken, the banks' boards could not make informed decisions about cases they were not familiar with. The credit risk officer estimated that only 3-4% of Handelsbanken's loan book are large and urgent loans that had to be approved by himself and the CEO, and even they were proposed by their local branch. In 2001, out of 400,000 credit decisions only 800 went to the board in Stockholm, of which only 40-50 were discussed by the full board (as opposed to the board's credit sub-committee). All other credit decisions were made at branch or regional level.

Unlike other banks Handelsbanken does not have special units that deal with loans in trouble. So the banker making a loan knows that if things go wrong he or she will be responsible and will have to deal with the situation until the loan has been repaid. It is hence not in the self-interest of anyone to support a large loan, even to a prestigious customer, if there is any doubt about the ability to repay.

Possible Risks of Autonomy

Given the high degree of autonomy of branches one might see them as franchises run by an independent entrepreneur, the branch manager. How can the bank make sure that the branch does not make wrong decisions? Should one not be concerned that the branch falls into one of two equally damaging extremes: either being lazy and unambitious, leaving a lot of good business on the table, or being too aggressive and giving customers prices that are too low and lending to borrowers that are too risky? These worries are certainly valid.

Many banks respond to them with a mix of micro-management and centralised decision making. For instance, it is quite common that relationship managers are given targets for how many times they need to see their clients physically, how many clients a relationship manager can have, what the branch budget can be for staff costs, etc. The unspoken reason, of course, is that the bank thinks the branch manager would come up with suboptimal decisions. This goes hand in hand with centralising decision making power such as bank-wide unified prices with little or no discretion for the branches. Equally, centralised credit systems can decide, often purely based on a computer system, whether a customer qualifies for a loan or not. In these cases the branch can do little to influence the decision either way. In short, in such banks branches become tightly managed sales organisations.

Plucky but prudent solutions

Handelsbanken would freely admit that not everything the branches do is automatically right. Where they would differ from their peers, however, is on the right remedy. Rather than taking away all decision making power that can be abused, they tend to stick to the view that the branch is in the best position to make these decisions. So, rather than relegate branches to mere sales offices, the bank works particularly hard to recruit the right staff, monitoring them quite closely (which we will discuss in the chapter on "Culture and Incentives") and coaching them frequently.

Arguably, the main function of the entire management layer of the regional banks, which are responsible for between 25 and 90 branches each, is to monitor and coach the branches.

So like other banks, Handelsbanken's management model starts from the fact that branches

“ Many banks undermine branch independence with a mix of micro-management and centralised decision making. ”

are important but not infallible. Yet they build this into a virtuous circle where managers are gradually given more and more responsibility as they develop, which has a strong motivational effect on staff. This, in turn, allows the bank to recruit and retain more capable branch personnel, who all take full responsibility for what is happening at their branch.

Other banks, by taking away responsibility and imposing decisions on the branches, deprive branch staff of that feeling of responsibility. After all, they did not decide that this customer should not get a loan when "computer says no" – so increasingly they do as they are told rather than what is right. Unsurprisingly, it is not one of the most uplifting moments in the life of branch staff to tell customers that they cannot do anything about a declined loan application, they do not know why it was declined. Or: sorry, they are not authorised to waive the overdraft fee that irritates a good customer. (Handelsbanken do not have many fees for everyday transactions, in particular not the many hidden penalty fees that make other banks quite a nice amount of money – the rationale is that customers hate such charges so the bank should not impose them).

Empire-building and the need to amass power is perhaps so common in banks, as in other organisations, that we do not notice these autocratic and centralising instincts any more. Perhaps it took a strong, if slightly eccentric, character like Jan Wallander to introduce a system at Handelsbanken that is diametrically opposed. Wallander became managing director in 1970 and put in place many of the elements described in this book. He wrote about his experience at the bank, and one of the most amusing parts of his account is about the resistance from managers who were more than keen for powers to be devolved from the centre to them – but who dug in their heels when it came to passing them on to lower organisational levels. They cited spurious grounds such as that people would not want additional responsibilities or that they lacked experience. Wallander continues that directors on the bank's board, many of them chief executives of large corporations, supported the whole process but were equally reluctant to start dealing with their local branch manager rather than the managing director.[36]

---

[36] Wallander (2004), pp. 39-41.

A Different Way of Thinking About Strategy

Handelsbanken's branches had historically been in Sweden, with some smaller regional presence in the other Scandinavian countries Denmark, Finland and Norway. It was hence a big step when in the early 2000s the bank decided to expand its presence in the United Kingdom, where the bank had had a small presence for decades, into a real regional bank. Handelsbanken's management had noted that the branch model works just as well outside Sweden in markets where it was possible to recruit very good bankers with a close cultural fit to the Handelsbanken model. In April 2008 the bank had 60 branches in the UK and had decided to split into two regional banks.

Conventional expansion

Much less talked about is the fact that similar international expansion operations are evolving in the Netherlands, Germany and Poland. The choice of these countries is remarkable as most other banks (at least those that I know) follow what may be termed a "portfolio model" when they decide on where to go next. In short, the portfolio model looks at the size, growth, competitiveness and profitability of banking in a large number of countries. Its default recommendation, with few qualitative changes, is for a bank to expand into large and growing banking markets with high profit margins.

This paradigm for international growth in banking is so widespread that many of the most prestigious management consultancies produce detailed banking profit pool analyses. The models of McKinsey & Company and of the Boston Consulting Group, for instance, allow you to see what the profit for all banks is in a given customer segment, product segment and country. You could see how much money can be made in selling credit cards to individuals in Russia and how fast this is growing, or how much money there is in loans to large companies in France. The underlying argument is that the difference in profit growth between banks is only to a small degree determined by how well the bank is run and to a much greater extent by the choice of markets. Banks that had a portfolio with many highly profitable, fast growing segments, so the argument goes, tended to experience fast profit growth. So if you want to grow profits you should set up shop in those segments where profits grow fast.

Problems

Now, when thinking about strategy there is nothing wrong with using this type of analysis as one among many other considerations.[37] The problem with using it as the only or the main strategy tool is simply that it tries to forecast things that may not be forecastable and largely leaves out equally important but much fuzzier aspects.

First, forecastability: I would argue that the development of banking profits over long time horizons is subject to a so-called Knightian uncertainty, i.e. an uncertainty that cannot be quantified. This does not mean that attempts to do so cannot be enlightening; but there is a risk of introducing pseudo-certainty.

Secondly, ignoring qualitative factors, which are crucially important. They should not be ignored simply because they cannot be quantified: what is your bank really good at? Would it be better than others at going into a particular market? Is there a cultural fit, would the new operations be manageable? For instance, I was not part of the decision making behind the forays of nearly all of Handelsbanken's peers into

---

[37] A lot more could be said about problems with this approach, for instance their self-defeating tendency (since so many banks use this approach they all go for supposedly profitable markets which end up with much more intense competition as the result of which they are less profitable than before).

Ukraine and Russia. But I would not be surprised to learn that an abundance of hard statistical facts about economic growth and bank profitability in these countries was allowed to outweigh qualitative considerations. At least I have never heard representatives of these banks discussing qualitative factors much when they presented these decisions.

Another fuzzy question that is hard to answer is what the cost can be if one of the portfolio investments goes wrong. The portfolio approach comes dressed like the sibling of a stock portfolio. But unlike a portfolio of stocks banks can lose much more than their initial investment if, for instance, they have provided additional funding to the subsidiary or there is an expectation that they would prop it up if things go wrong.

Handelsbanken's strategic thought process

Therefore, Handelsbanken's completely different strategic choice first puzzled, then impressed me. Discussions with managers, the business head for Handelsbanken International, and the head of one of the regional banks in the UK clarified Handelsbanken's thought process for me.

It revolves around how similar the business culture is to Sweden's; whether one can find branch managers with a similar "philosophical" outlook and qualification; and whether there is an unmet customer need for what Handelsbanken has to offer.

To take the UK as an example, an important element behind the decision to grow there was the realisation that there were many very good companies that were not terribly pleased with the decision by their bank to serve them via call centres or an ever-changing sequence of relationship managers.

Branches are opened only where the bank can recruit a branch manager who has a good knowledge of the local area and represents a strong cultural fit with the Handelsbanken philosophy. In France, for instance, a lack of cultural fit has been a major reason not to expand further. It is also one of many obstacles to developing a presence in Russia or Ukraine, where the business customs are not compatible with the Handelsbanken approach.

Implementing that strategy in a thousand little steps

Crucially, too, there was never a strategic big bang but successive trial and error decisions.[38] The bank opened a branch or two, let them run for some time, discussed with the branch managers what their experience was, then if things were promising it would open a few more branches and wait again for a couple of years.

The newly recruited branch manager starts with a fairly low discretion limit for lending and is paired with a Handelsbanken risk officer. Branch managers learn that they ruin their career if they produce loan losses (Ulf Riese, the chief financial officer, likes to say 'we hate loan losses' as though there is really nothing to justify them – we will come back to this point in the next chapter). The new branch starts out doing business with companies that are owned by Scandinavian companies or have similar links. Such a piecemeal approach is fairly low risk – and it is not one for chief executives who want to transform the organisation they run. It is what you would do if you wanted to do the right thing over a hundred year period, not if you wanted something to show in three or at most five years.

---

[38] There have been temptations in Handelsbanken's history, especially in the good times when its competitors were expanding much faster, to jump ahead, but overall the bank has been fairly faithful to its roots. It is my understanding, for example, that former chairman Lars Grönstedt was advocating that the bank take a more active role in opening up Eastern European banking. The board, however, sided with chief executive Pär Boman, which led to Grönstedt's departure.

Successes

The results of this branch-based model are encouraging for those with long-term goals but no philosopher's stone to turn straw or bank branches or anything else into gold. Handelsbanken's experience of the average branch performance is very similar across the bank and quite similar between Sweden and other countries: it costs about five million Swedish crowns to open a new branch (including the cost before the branch reaches break-even), and each branch increases its annual profit by approximately three million crowns every year. In other words, the branches become more and more profitable over time, and while this analysis has been carried out including branches that are twenty or more years old there is no tendency for the profit per branch to stop growing at some point. In addition, the Handelsbanken branches in most countries, not just Sweden, rank

> **"** Handelsbanken has grown internationally in markets that no longer grow much, and had a good performance in countries where banks are in dire straits (for instance Denmark and the UK). **"**

ahead of their main competitors in terms of customer satisfaction as well as staff satisfaction.

This is not limited to Scandinavian markets. In the UK, the loyalty and satisfaction of both corporate and individual customers at Handelsbanken is significantly higher than at any of the large four UK banks. The research agency conducting the test even decided to break out the Handelsbanken results from the rest of the industry because they were such an outlier. (See Figure 4 overleaf.)

In other words, a strategic development that concentrates on qualitative aspects and prefers the trial-and-error approach has worked

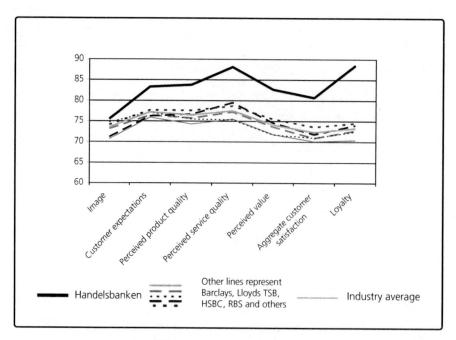

Figure 4: Customer satisfaction UK corporate banking[39]

rather well compared to what the "portfolio approach" would have recommended: Handelsbanken has grown internationally in markets that no longer grow much, and it has had a good performance in countries where banks are in dire straits (for instance Denmark and the UK).

In contrast, of the twelve best practice examples that one consulting company (no, I won't say which) recommended two years ago, most have performed very badly and five have hit the wall altogether. Perhaps HBOS, Fortis, Citi and Anglo Irish were not so successful after all, and recommendations such as growing non-prime lending may not have been quite as clever as they seemed back then.

---

[39] I am grateful to EPSI Research Services for the use of their data here. The graph shown is for corporate customers; the results for individual customers are very similar.

The instruments to fly on auto pilot

I have discussed two broad positions – empowerment of the branches rather than centralisation and micro-management; and going for step-by-step growth in areas of cultural affinity rather than big bang market entries. Now we will look more closely at the way the branches interact with their regional bank and with central product areas.

Dialogue not targets

The relationship between a regional bank and its branches is defined by a precise allocation of costs and benefits to the branches and a continued dialogue about branch performance. It is not defined, as in many other banks, by business targets and priorities that are cascaded down and that the branch has to achieve.

The Handelsbanken way appears easier as it does away with the whole planning process. Yet it is actually fairly time and resource consuming, because it requires very good management reporting systems. Take the allocation of costs and benefits. There is of course an ongoing dialogue about the costs for IT developments and for regulatory projects which Handelsbanken has to undertake bank-wide, for which costs are allocated to the branches. Similarly, when I started following the bank there was a lot of debate about the revenues the branches received for selling asset management or investment banking products. The allocation mechanism has since been adjusted so that the bulk of revenues now goes to the branches rather than the supporting central product units.

The trickiest allocation decision has to do with funding and capital. If a branch takes in savings deposits on which it pays 2% interest and uses this money to make loans on which it receives 4%, how much of the difference is income on the deposits and how much on the loan? It gets even more complicated: usually deposits can be withdrawn at relatively short notice (short maturities) whereas loans tend to have longer maturities of up to several years. Evidently there is a risk attached to this and also an offsetting income since interest rates on long maturities tend to be higher. This is what is often referred to as the income from "maturity transformation", i.e. from banks' borrowing money over shorter maturities than they lend. Handelsbanken as a whole does not want the branches to start speculating in this way, attracting vast amounts of short maturity deposits and making long maturity loans – see deadly sin number one. The traditional way to solve this is to insert an internal bank for the branches, the so-called treasury department. It pays the branches an interest rate for their customer deposits (the branches "give" the money to the central treasury) and charges them a different price for funds to make loans with longer maturities to branch customers.

Handelsbanken have invested much time and effort to make sure that the branches get a rate both on loans and deposits that corresponds to their actual maturities as well as the actual funding costs of the bank. This is a particularly important point since some branches make more loans than they have deposits, and the treasury department needs to find the funding to plug the gap.

Sometimes there is a bank-wide gap, which is the case for nearly all Scandinavian banks. Customers tend to have their savings in mutual funds, life insurance policies and other investments that are not deposits and which, therefore, cannot be used by banks to fund their lending. Then the treasury department needs to borrow this money from other banks or other investors, e.g. pension funds or insurance companies (collectively called "wholesale funding" as opposed to funding banks get from their customers' deposits).

The price of funding in wholesale markets is infinitely more complex than in our toy example of the 2% deposit and the 4% loan. The cost of wholesale funding, for instance, varies considerably for different types of loans to be financed: wholesale funding for mortgages is often much cheaper. In the Handelsbanken branches this is all more or less reflected in the branch reporting. Funding costs charged by the treasury unit vary by maturity, whether the product to be funded is itself liquid or not (for instance a loan to a customer) and whether a loan is backed by a mortgage and can be used to issue cheaper covered bonds.

This has three effects. The vast majority of actual income is allocated to the branches rather than reported in a central treasury department. The bank as well as investors know that what they see reported as the income for the branches is really from business with customers rather than from maturity transformation. It rules out the inclusion of any income from asset/liability mismatches in reported branch figures, and so takes away the incentive to speculate. And the branches accept the prices they get by the internal treasury as "real", in other words branch managers have no excuse for weak performance. Handelsbanken knows that branch autonomy and internal competitions work only if you take away all excuses for branch managers. In other words decentralisation requires reported figures that are accurate and widely accepted.

Capital care

A similar fine-tuning in the internal allocation takes place when it comes to bank capital. Capital is meant to cover unexpected losses, so the branch should hold more capital for riskier loans. The bank has spent a lot of effort to make sure this really happens, i.e. that the branch knows that for every different customer it will get a different amount of capital allocated. Regional banks get capital allocated for their business and are competing against each other on the return on capital.

At the branch level things are kept a bit simpler by charging a cost for each unit of capital the branch consumes.

For readers who do not have a banking background this may well sound remarkably trivial and common sense (if so it would be another good reason for having more non-bankers run banks).[40] As much as they try, many banks, however, find that the devil is in the detail, and they often encounter some of the following problems.

Perhaps the most benign is that branch staff simply ignore the allocations of funding costs and capital if they think that the system comes up with nonsensical results, if it is too complex to understand, or changes too often. To get to this point does not take much. Wholesale funding costs, for instance, can change very quickly (even before the credit crunch) so it must seem very puzzling for someone in a branch that he or she could make a loan for 4% on Friday but should charge 5% just a week later. Of course it is similarly problematic to leave internal prices, say for mortgages, unchanged when the real price for the bank changes. Handelsbanken found that it was at times difficult for their branches with accurate prices to do business, when another bank's branches were still selling mortgages at last month's cheaper prices.

A more serious problem arises if someone in the organisation decides to use the treasury department pricing list for other purposes as well. Let us say the bank overall wants to attract more deposits, so someone in head office might come up with the idea to pay the branches a bit more for customer deposits than they would otherwise receive. Innocent as this might seem, it very often leads to confusion, because now nobody can tell how much money the bank really makes with deposits and where the marketing cost of paying the branches a bit more has

---

[40] Interestingly, the team around Jan Wallander that developed many elements of the Handelsbanken philosophy described in this book were not originally bankers but researchers or businessmen. (Wallander 2004, p. 37).

gone. At some point the branches will realise that someone is playing games with them and they will start talking about the official treasury department prices and the real prices in the way that people in some emerging countries talk about official and real, black market exchange rates.

Perhaps most serious is the situation where people in the branches start gambling with the system. As a consultant I once had a client (one of the bluest blue chip banks in Europe) where branch staff had found out that they would get more income and less capital costs allocated if they split a loan into two separate products – which combined were absolutely identical to the original loan but were treated differently by internal systems!

A system developed, refined, explained, and always analysing and improving

In short, it is not remarkable that Handelsbanken wanted to have a good system for accurate allocation of income and costs. What is remarkable is the amount of time and effort they devoted to developing, refining and explaining the system. This was because they really wanted a process that worked by itself and did not need repeated intervention – a process where the branches automatically did the right things. Their view was that 'you have to take away all possible excuses for the branches', such as wrong reporting systems, if you want them to perform.

At the same time, the bank is keen to have controlling systems that allow the regional banks to monitor and supervise the branches. One element here is the review of credit applications for larger loans. The idea is not that more competent people higher up in the organisation take the decision, but to ensure that the branch follow the credit policy.

Another element of monitoring the branches is an annual branch audit. An internal audit team visits each branch and examines everything from branch appearance to HR practices at the branch. The audit also focuses closely on the quality of documentation, as Handelsbanken have found that proper documentation can be key to recovering a loan. The branch gets a grade between 1 and 5 from the audit team. The audit report is an important basis for the discussion between the branch manager and the regional bank. Having a bad audit grade for several years is likely to end a career as branch manager.

Handelsbanken's controlling systems also include detailed measurements of branch activities. These activity measures are discussed between the branch and the regional bank. In addition, they have played an important role in identifying efficiency improvement potential, which will be discussed below.

It is this rejection of new grand designs in favour of constant small improvements that sets Handelsbanken apart. We will encounter it time and again when comparing them to their competition.

Finesse

Handelsbanken is still tweaking its reporting systems, three and a half decades after Jan Wallander joined the bank. This shows that despite the fundamental simplicity of the Handelsbanken model it can still take a lot of work and effort to get things right. It is necessary to put all this effort into perfecting all the elements of the model, as they are connected and would not work without each other. Incremental international growth requires a working branch model which in turn requires a controlling and reporting system that is well thought through. The model can function like a plane on autopilot, but only if all components and instruments work well. And what it also requires is the right culture, which will be the focus of the next chapter.

6

Culture and Incentives

One of the difficult things in banking is to distinguish prudence from timidity. If a bank does not take part in a fast growing, profitable market where its competitors are raking in money, is that a sign of admirable caution or being too conservative and undynamic? It is a question that applies to individual people within the bank but also one that investors in a bank have to ask themselves. We will first try to describe how Handelsbanken deals with this challenge internally, before looking at the communication between the bank and its investors in a separate chapter.

What the Branch Staff Say

I have talked to numerous branch managers, as well as to staff. What they say is consistent.

Self-direction

What all of them found motivating was to be fairly self-directed and entrepreneurial. Especially for those who had worked for other banks before, it was a liberating feeling to be able to choose which clients to serve, whom to visit in person, what to offer clients. This compares with the more prescriptive environment in a number of other banks, where these decisions are taken centrally. One new branch manager showed nearly childish joy that after a long stint in a corporate environment he could be an entrepreneur himself, selecting the right location for his new branch, recruiting the people he wanted and taking all the other decisions that someone starting a small company would take. But there was also a sense in day-to-day business that the organisation acted reasonably and that the culture was supporting and not hindering branch activities. This applied particularly to lending decisions, where the bank was seen as conservative but fact based and rational – not cutting all exposure to certain sectors or abandoning long standing clients.

Client contact

Another aspect that came up frequently was the ability to deal with clients directly. One corporate banker and one personal banker in the UK both explained how frustrating it had been that their previous employers had decided that large swathes of clients should no longer have their personal contact person. Work is more personalised at Handelsbanken and the bankers generally felt this enabled them to provide better service.

There is some enjoyment at having broad responsibility for anything that touches one's customers. This is not the division of labour that assigns staff a number of repetitive tasks. There are few hard and fast procedures. Rather, Handelsbanken people are responsible for doing whatever a customer situation calls for. It is customary for clients to be given the mobile phone number of their relationship banker. If a wealthy client wants a loan for 120% of the price of a property he is buying, there is no rule saying that those loans are capped at 75%. If, taking everything into consideration, the branch is happy to lend to the customer, they can do so (unless the total amount exceeds their credit limit, so the next level also needs to be comfortable with the loan). But if things go wrong, the banker who made the loan is also responsible for recovering the amount. One can see that this job profile is more appealing and satisfying to intelligent people.

Stability

A third observation, again mostly from people with a background in other banks, was the stability of the structure and the organisation, whereas at their old banks they had experienced regular reorganisations. My impression was that people enjoyed spending most of their time thinking about customer business rather than changes (and inevitably politics) at their bank.

Responsibility breeds satisfaction – for employees and customers

The overall impression one gets from Handelsbanken staff is that they quite enjoy what they are doing. Nobody ever brought up the compensation system as a negative – they all seemed to derive their motivation from their work itself rather than the expectation of a big pay cheque. They may not be financial whiz kids, but they seem good at what they are doing. Based on the statistically highly insignificant sample of one, when I look at my customer relationship with the bank it is clear that they are all extremely eager to make life easy for me as a customer. And they generally succeed.

It is difficult to define what a strong corporate culture is but you know it when you see it. Staff in different functions and regions give very similar reports about how things are done and what the bank's priorities are – all in their own words, making it improbable they could be parroting any party line. In discussion, Handelsbanken staff often refer back to events in the bank's history, and "story telling" generally plays an important role. Rarely have I heard so many amusing and instructive anecdotes from bankers. Many of them have spent their entire career with the bank. This gives the organisation a cohesive identity around the Handelsbanken management model and differentiates it quite clearly from other banks. Importantly, the

Handelsbanken model is not seen as static and does not serve as an argument for inertia. The practice of internet banking for each branch shows that the bank is capable of moving with the times in a way that is true to its philosophy. In the chapter on risk management we will see how some change is actually legitimised by the bank's heritage, by 'making the Bank more Handelsbanken'.

Mechanisms

Informal

Handelsbanken staff enjoy their job, so they are motivated to do good work without the promise of a bonus. This is reinforced by another factor that recurs throughout Handelsbanken's way of working: simplicity.[41] The organisational primacy of the branch as a fairly autonomous unit with only a handful of staff may not be the most industrially efficient solution. But apart from motivating staff it also makes it relatively easy to observe individual behaviour and performance. In a self-contained unit of often fewer than ten people it is not terribly difficult to see if someone is shirking, and to take corrective action, often quite informally.

Formal

Talking about more formal mechanisms, Handelsbanken relies on internal competition between branches and regions. Performance data such as the cost:income ratio are published for all units and especially within groups of comparable branches (i.e. branches of similar size, business mix and age) and then ranked. Handelsbanken have even

---

[41] Wallander (2004), pp. 9-10.

created performance metrics that I at least had never heard of – "internal market shares", or the share that one unit has in the overall group context. The regional manager of the region around Stockholm surprised me at our first meeting by talking about his Mid-Sweden region's internal market share. At our next meeting, he showed me figures that demonstrated how much his region was ahead of others in its uptake of a voluntary

> **It is quite refreshing that the main topics for boasting are how much money one has not spent and not lost.**

staff incentive programme. Nearly everyone talks about the quality of loans they make or are responsible for. So the transparency of internal rankings and benchmarking can quickly become the court of shame for someone who made a loan to a shaky customer who subsequently went bankrupt. Having made imprudent loans or just loans that were not beyond doubt seems to be the best way to limit one's career in the bank.

It is quite refreshing that the main topics for boasting – within the bounds of Scandinavian egalitarianism and modesty – are not how much money one has made personally or for the bank, but how much money one has not spent (low cost:income ratio) and how much money one has not lost (good loan quality).

It would seem logical that a bank focuses on the downside, not the upside. After all, when you a make a loan you can earn just one or two per cent if all goes well but lose a hundred per cent if things go wrong. But for a long time, Handelsbanken was in the minority among optimistic, enthusiastic banks. Its creed is not to lose money. It applies the same yardstick to its customers. In the words of the chief risk officer, Handelsbanken lends not to those 'who want to be rich or need money' but to those 'who don't want to be poor or don't need money'.

The bank is relatively good at collecting data for benchmarking purposes – benchmarking branches or regions against each other as well as against the competition or the overall market (the regional manager mentioned above also knew what the number of corporate insolvencies in his region had been and was fairly proud that Handelsbanken in his region had a much lower share of insolvent customers than its overall lending market share would imply). Refining these measurements is an ongoing process.

At Handelsbanken the effort other banks might put into strategic planning and budgeting goes into refining control and reporting tools so that all levels have the right information on a timely basis. This includes visibility of performance to the next higher organisational level, which allows ongoing monitoring.

The point of this measuring and ranking is on the one hand to motivate people (in a rather cost-effective way), and on the other to identify a given unit's strengths and weaknesses. Former CEO Wallander describes in his book how he would visit the branches once a year – given the growth in the number of branches this is now primarily done by the regional managers. In discussions with the branches they often noted that benchmarking is a valuable diagnostic tool to identify weaknesses and opportunities.

Incentives

No bonuses

As already stated, Handelsbanken does not award bonuses. With one exception, nobody in the senior management team and nobody in the branch operations either in Sweden or outside gets paid more or less depending on performance. The one exception is some staff members in the smaller Asset Management and Capital Markets product divisions, where competitive pressure forces the bank to share some profit with staff. The only general form of variable compensation is the additional allocation to the group's pension scheme in the form of the Oktogonen foundation, in which each member of staff from chief executive to clerical staff has an equal stake. The bank allocates money to the foundation if its return on equity in a given period exceeds that of its peers. Yet even here there is no reward for individual performance, and the Oktogonen foundation is not positioned as a bonus element but as sharing profits fairly with employees.

This system embodies the bank's visceral dislike for risk-taking, its focus on concentrating on customer satisfaction over profits, and its emphasis on long-term orientation. As the system has been in place for a very long time, there is simply no expectation of any special remuneration for doing the job well. Staff know that they will get a competitive salary and a very generous pension from the Oktogonen foundation once they retire.

Job stability and progress

Another important cultural element is an implicit job guarantee. The bank tends to find jobs in other areas of the bank for employees who are strictly speaking redundant. This makes it easier for staff willingly to lose market share when the risk/reward balance would not be right, or to suggest efficiency improvements that render their job unnecessary.

It is also rare that senior positions get filled externally (with the exception of branch manager hires in new geographical areas). Careers are made within the bank. At the end of 2008, the 29 most senior people in the bank had on average been with the bank for 23 years – only two had worked at Handelsbanken for less than ten years.

Apart from job satisfaction, the key motivation for doing well is that good performance will be rewarded with promotions within the bank.

> **At the end of 2008, the 29 most senior people in the bank had on average been with the bank for 23 years.**

The rules are fairly clear and stable about what constitutes good performance (low costs, low credit losses, doing better than peers, etc) so the unwritten contract between the bank and the employee is credible. Promotion can thus replace cash incentives as the main tool for staff motivation.

Change is moderate and evolutionary, and there is no large scale restructuring. The lack of restructuring or of shifts in corporate strategy forms the cornerstone for the system of internal promotion. You cannot have competition as the main motivational tool in an organisation that frequently changes its structure or management. If staff know that there is a high likelihood that the rules and the jury will change over the next five years they will demand more immediate and tangible reward than an implicit promise for future promotion. In this way a lack of organisational stability tends to force banks into a bonus culture.

Implications

Handelsbanken may be a good place to work, but it is not necessarily one where underperformers keep their job. After Pär Boman became chief executive in 2006 a number of people were replaced. This was done discreetly – apparently the bank does not believe in the power of public sacking, so people were moved within the organisation to other, sometimes more ceremonial, roles or accepted outside offers.

In general, however, there is a tendency for people to stay in their roles for much longer than in other banks, and they also certainly stay longer with their employer. Having people with considerable experience in their job is desirable where staff have broad responsibilities. Having bankers who were essentially in the same job in the last banking crisis or the last recession can be helpful. It is similarly useful for a corporate culture that values constant incremental improvements – people know what would constitute an improvement, and they know they will have to live for a long time with any changes they make. In addition, relatively flat hierarchies remove the incentive for ruthless self-advancement. A successful branch manager can become head of a region – yet this itself is not radically different to running a branch. The bank does not employ people who only do their job in order to be promoted to something else.

Empowering people necessitates a strict selection of staff, on the basis of cultural fit as well as qualifications. People involved with the international branch expansion unequivocally name finding the right people to lead branches as the biggest obstacle. Apart from finding competent bankers who fit the Handelsbanken philosophy of low risk, high touch local banking, it is time consuming to coach these new people during their first years.

The workplace at Handelsbanken is not a temporarily advantageous union of mercenaries driven by high rewards. Neither is it the setting for palace intrigues where careers rise on political skills and by subjugating the long-term well-being of the organisation to tactical and particular interests (cf. Ferguson's quote on page 64). Instead, it has more of the ethos of a well-functioning 19th century civil service. The staff are not geniuses perhaps, but talented and moderately ambitious people who are motivated to do what is right because it is right, not because it earns them a financial reward. For staff the system has the great attraction of entrepreneurial autonomy, a more interesting and satisfying job, though at the expense of more limited financial rewards. Customers get a motivated and capable contact person for all their banking needs – even if the bank is not the most cutting edge partner for financial engineering and risk-taking and can occasionally say no to its customers. Shareholders may have to forgo the quick dollar (or Swedish crown) every now and then, but they know that the bank is run well and that nobody has the mindset nor the motivation for betting the bank.

7

Risk Management

Handelsbanken's Approach to Risk Management

Philosophy

Handelsbanken's core philosophy is to take risks only in those areas where they have demonstrable strengths, and to reduce all other risks as much as economically possible. Its risk management is organised accordingly, with credit risk, where the bank sees its competitive advantage, handled mostly in a decentralised way and most other risks in a more centralised way. The responsibility for lending lies first and foremost with the branches. Larger loans involve a review of the loan application by the regional bank or even the central organisation in Stockholm – but they merely veto or validate what the branch intends to do. Well over half (57%) of loans by number are decided at branch level, 35% are reviewed at regional bank level, and only 8% are also reviewed by the credit committee in Stockholm or the entire board.

Reviews

The intention of these reviews is not to transfer the decision making to more competent people. Rather, it is to give the regional banks and the centre a tool to monitor whether the branches are following the bank's credit policy correctly and applying good judgement. Reviews do not take away a case from the branch, they merely try to ensure that the branch performs a thorough and balanced review in line with the bank's credit policy. It is particularly important to keep the branch firmly in charge since a loan application pays close attention not just to financial ratios but also to qualitative factors which only the branch can judge properly. Handelsbanken's CEO likes to say that the quantitative analysis is the easy but not the most important part of the credit analysis.

The branch, which nearly always means the same relationship manager who made the loan, also retains responsibility for the customer if things go wrong and the loan has to be restructured or handled as a workout case. There is an offer of help from the centre but no separate problem workout unit. The centre does not tell the branches which customer groups to lend to or not to lend to, and it does not impose any volume targets or restrictions. There are, it is true, frequent exchanges of ideas and opinions, for instance in the format of a branch visit by the regional manager or the chief executive. Even here, however, the bank emphasises a non-hierarchical and relatively open dialogue.

Customers-first, portfolio second

For all lending decisions the focus is on default risk only, in other words one does not accept somewhat higher risks for higher margins. This goes hand in hand with a very individualistic assessment of each customer: the bank is happy to lend even large amounts to those that are creditworthy. It does not follow the approach of many other banks that look at a portfolio as a whole: another lender may take a portfolio of, say, credit card loans and accept that 5% of the loans will default if it is possible to charge an interest rate that compensates for this loss. In contrast, Handelsbanken believes that there is no such thing as a homogenous portfolio of loans; each borrower is different. Hence one can get a good assessment of the solidity of one customer but cannot reliably forecast how difficult times affect a portfolio with which one is only familiar on a portfolio level. According to the bank's credit risk officer, portfolio adherents had warned the bank of its sizeable loan concentration to the textile sector, which was considered risky. Yet none of Handelsbanken's clients in this sector defaulted, raising the question why one would want to follow a portfolio approach to direct new lending when one can make use of the much richer information of looking at each customer individually.

The development of Handelsbanken's credit portfolio during the Swedish banking crisis is instructive. Compared to the Swedish banking system overall, Handelsbanken was only moderately underweighted in the problem sectors such as lending to finance companies or real estate related lending. Portfolio weights explain only 14% of the difference in loan losses between Handelsbanken and its competitors; 86% are due to better customer selection.[42]

Avoidance policies

One lesson from the banking crisis in the early 1990s was the danger of lending to non-bank financial companies. It is today company credit policy not to lend money to companies that are in the business of lending money themselves. Handelsbanken has also avoided funding SIVs and conduits. There has been one unhappy exception where the bank became liquidity provider to the SIV of a US investment bank which promptly ran into trouble. While the scale of the problem is fairly small, my impression is that this experience served as a powerful reminder to everyone in the bank how important it is to stick to the time-honoured principles of the Handelsbanken way.

For most other forms of risk Handelsbanken tries to keep their management away from the branches and to reduce them as much as

---

[42] I owe these impressive numbers to the analysis in Lindgren/Wallander/Sjöberg (1994), pp. 67-180.

economically feasible. On liquidity risk, for instance, the bank has from 2006 extended the maturity structure of its liabilities in order to reduce its balance sheet maturity mismatch. While this is not easily visible, the development of quarterly net interest income (Figure 5 below) shows that the contribution from non-customer business has decreased significantly. This is shown in the "Other" area in the chart, as opposed to the dark portion, "Regional banks", which represents net interest income from customer lending and deposit taking. The graph also shows how Handelsbanken's net interest income from customer activities starts growing strongly with the financial crisis as the bank is winning back share in a market with strongly rising margins.

According to the bank, SEK 600 million net interest income from asset liability mismatches fell away and had to be replaced with customer-driven income. (For liquidity risk is not a risk category they want to compete in, even if it does generate SEK 600m.)

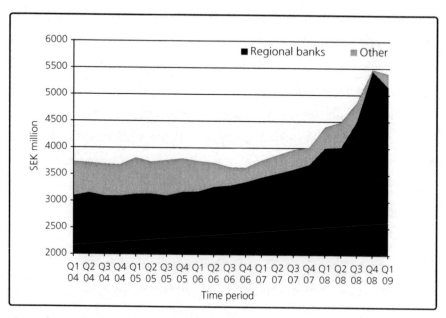

Figure 5: Handelsbanken net interest income

Similarly, one does not find significant mismatches of interest rates or currencies on Handelsbanken's balance sheet, nor its customers'. Other banks routinely take positions (on and off balance sheet) on the movement of interest rates which can contribute a large share of net interest income. Handelsbanken does not spend much time and resources on forecasting rates or currency movements. Rather, since they do not expect to be better at it than others or than their investors, they try to keep the balance sheet so closely matched that the net impact of any move is more or less neutral.

Treasury Operations Without a Profit Mandate

An important step in that direction was the decision to make the group treasury a function without a profit objective.[43] The aim of the treasury function is to fund the branch operations while keeping risks from asset and liability mismatches to a minimum.

The bank engages in maturity transformation only with assets that are de facto sticky – i.e. household savings – not with corporate or institutional deposits or wholesale funding. As a result, the liabilities on Handelsbanken's balance sheet have a maturity that is only slightly lower than that of its assets. This was a challenge when other banks were running significant funding mismatches and competing on the basis of cheaper, albeit riskier, funding. Today Handelsbanken is

---

[43] The economist John Kay declared that at Halifax, the UK building society where he had been a board member, 'the road to nemesis began [...] on the day it was decided that treasury should be a profit centre in its own right rather than an ancillary activity.' (*Financial Times*, September 24th, 2008.)

unfazed by new liquidity regulation forcing banks to reduce their funding mismatches since unlike many of its peers it never had any.

Risk averse

In the past, the treasury function had about half its staff working as proprietary traders, taking bets on different interest rate scenarios with the aim to make an additional profit for the bank. This was completely abandoned a few years ago – an example of how the bank continues to implement the "Handelsbanken philosophy" more and more rigorously. When funding markets dried up, especially since September 2008, its risk-averse funding approach started to bear fruit.

First, the earlier decision to lengthen maturities of wholesale funding meant that the bank did not have to roll over large amounts.

Second, Handelsbanken was one of the first banks to publish its liquidity position, which showed that during the crisis the bank had been issuing mortgage bonds continuously. In fact it was awash with liquidity and a net lender to its peer banks, the overall banking system and the Swedish government. The fact that it thus did not need money further increased its reputation as a safe haven and its treasury group could rely on investors asking to fund the bank (so-called reverse enquiries).

When the European banking system was dangerously short of US dollars it was also among the few European banks that could raise substantial funding in the US market. Swap prices reflecting the dollar shortage of European banks that were shut out of the US market meant that after swapping these amounts into Swedish crowns the bank obtained funding below STIBOR rates[44], i.e. cheaper than before the financial crisis.

---

[44] The Stockholm interbank rates in Swedish crowns, i.e. the Swedish equivalent of LIBOR rates.

Risk wise

The bank continued to play a sophisticated signalling role by being the first Nordic bank after the Lehman insolvency to issue longer dated bonds again. Credit markets rewarded the low risk profile of Handelsbanken so the bank had the cheapest funding costs of the Nordic banks. Its credit default swap spread was below those of all other Nordic banks, and for some time even lower than that of the Swedish government. Minimising funding risks and forgoing treasury profits thus cost money during the good years but has come to pay off substantially since the credit crunch began.

No casino

A cultural aversion to market risk also means that the investment banking (capital markets) division executes orders for customers and does some market making but does not take any speculative or proprietary positions; those it still had were sold. In banking terminology, it is nearly exclusively customer driven and a "flow" business. Business in this field is overall fairly stable. Unfortunately investors cannot see from published financial accounts how Handelsbanken's investment banking differs from those of other banks that do more proprietary trading – IFRS reporting standards do not distinguish between the source of investment banking income. In the published accounts of Handelsbanken (and any other bank) the fairly stable and low risk customer flow business is shown in the same way as the more volatile, riskier speculative position taking.[45] But the fact that Handelsbanken's investment banking produces rather stable, low

---

[45] It is unfortunate that even in Handelsbanken's reporting the capital markets division includes results from operations which the division undertakes for the bank rather than its customers. It was spread-widening on the liquidity portfolio that caused the volatility in the reported quarterly profits of the division during 2008, not the customer business.

risk profits shows how simplistic it is to claim that investment banking is "casino banking".

Emerging markets

Assuming only risks the bank really understands, and in many cases better than anyone else, has also meant that Handelsbanken has been extremely cautious in expanding into emerging markets. Among the large Scandinavian banks it is the only one that does not have a significant presence in Eastern Europe (it has one branch each in Estonia, Moscow and St. Petersburg, dealing with Scandinavian clients, and eleven branches in Poland). The chief executive once explained to me that this was seen as too much of a macro bet on the development of these countries – and why would Handelsbanken know better about it than others?

On the other hand, where there is demand for the type of banking Handelsbanken offers there, it follows its traditional trial-and-error approach, opening a few pilot branches at a time.

Organisational Aspects of Risk Management

Handelsbanken's risk organisation and its treasury set up are formal mechanisms to avoid several of the seven deadly sins. Culture plays another important role – we have already discussed in the previous chapter that the organisation values loyalty to the Handelsbanken model and abhors credit losses. These values are stronger than those put on profit or growth. This shows that the Handelsbanken culture does not encourage individual staff members to act imprudently. It is perfectly acceptable in this bank to lose market share and report shrinking volumes and profits in a bull market. It is not acceptable to engage in riskier lending even if this might bring in large profits. Unlike other banks, where people are rewarded and promoted if a risky gamble turns out well, Handelsbanken staff are usually aware that imprudent lending is career-limiting and not rewarded – even if things go well.

Institutional memory

Another cultural or organisational feature in Handelsbanken's risk management is its long "institutional memory". It is a consequence of the fairly simple organisational structure described above: people stay with the bank for a long time, and in their roles for longer than at other banks. The organisation collectively benefits from vivid memories of how things have gone wrong in the past, and hence what one should avoid or, if it happens despite all precaution, what works to solve the problem.

This stands in marked contrast to my personal experience in many other banks. In one large bank, people and structures changed so often and so quickly that it was hard to find out if the bank had tried something before and what the experience had been. Constant restructuring left people with very limited experience in their job, at best a vague idea of what other organisational units were doing, and often no access to their predecessors. Despite the fact that the bank had over three hundred years of history, many of its staff had access to an institutional memory of no more than two or three years. 'Disasters happen when the last man who can remember what happened last time has retired'.[46] So it must be desirable to keep memories of past crises, but also simply of individual cases gone wrong, fresh in the institutional memory for as long as possible. Handelsbanken's credit risk officer once remarked that the reason for leaving the risk organisation substantially unchanged for the past fifteen years is that 'everybody knows what to do'.

---

[46] Mervyn King in a speech of March 17th, 2009, paraphrasing the journalist Christopher Filde.

Institutional contrarianism

We have already mentioned that most activities in banking, and financial services more broadly, have a more complex temporal nature than manufacturing or selling widgets. Financial activities can produce handsome profits over several years before making a sizeable loss, though some others have a more regular pattern, i.e. lower profits but also no spectacular losses. The challenge is to distinguish between the two, or more precisely to avoid the trap of extrapolating from one or a few periods of good profits. In his *General Theory of Employment, Interest and Money* (1937) John Maynard Keynes describes the temptation to assume that the current state of affairs reflects the likelihood of different future scenarios correctly and that general opinion is more accurate than one's own, which leads to what we may call "group think" and what Keynes calls 'conventional' opinions. Handelsbanken's strong culture and identity make it easier for them to come to the conclusion that other banks have simply got it wrong, even collectively wrong, thereby eschewing imprudent activities even when they are yielding rich profits. Other Nordic and international banks have remarked in private that they see Handelsbanken as a very different, even awkward, institution that does things quite differently. This environment makes it internally easier to form an independent opinion even where this is at odds with received wisdom.

Capital in a crisis

Coming back to the last of the seven deadly sins and the mistaken trust in good financial ratios, it is interesting that Handelsbanken has warned that capital is there for bad times. Its view is that very solid capital ratios during good times do not signify that the bank is overcapitalised.

As a result, the bank's capital planning is based on a real crisis scenario (among others, a repeat of the Swedish banking crisis 1991/2). In Scandinavia Handelsbanken was the first bank to define its capital target under the new regulatory regime of Basel II.

When there was a general feeling that banks could reduce their capital, Handelsbanken "disappointed" investors by setting a very high target corridor for its tier I ratio of 9–11% (when the regulatory minimum was 4%). Unlike investors, the bank realised that the capital ratios that matter are those in the most difficult and stressed environment. By implication, capital ratios in good times do not reveal much about banks' absolute or relative solidity.

Harnessing competition but keeping risks under control

Combining our findings with those from the chapter on Handelsbanken's strategy and business focus, it is fair to say that the bank starts with a decision on risk appetite and takes growth and profit largely as a function of this risk appetite and prevailing market conditions.

Banks compete not just on price or service quality but also on risk appetite. In the short term, it is often profitable to go up the risk curve. This usually involves one or the other of the seven deadly sins. This behaviour leads to an increase in reported profits with the increase in risk remaining largely invisible in the reports. Therefore, any competition in banking has an inbuilt tendency towards higher risks.

Handelsbanken's internal competitions and its competition in the marketplace with other banks work only because they are kept in check by its a priori decisions on risk. This includes the risk philosophy that the bank accepts only credit risk and minimises all other forms of risk. It also depends on a credit policy that is not changed through the credit cycle and is taken very seriously. Competition is a powerful force but in order to harness it the risk appetite has to be fixed first.[47]

A real end to boom and bust

In the upswing of the business cycle Handelsbanken's unique approach implies losing market share and lower profit growth than its competitors. This is because the bank's risk appetite has not changed and it is not willing to participate in the riskier segments that drive the credit expansion, but it is suffering from the market-wide contraction of margins. In the downturn, when other banks reduce their lending excessively, Handelsbanken's unchanged risk appetite means that they can pick up market share at higher margins.

This countercyclical behaviour underlines that Handelsbanken's approach is diametrically opposed to that of most other banks. Other banks nearly always have profit targets, while Handelsbanken refuses to do any planning and forecasting – but instead makes explicit decisions about its risk appetite. This means that other banks will eagerly participate in the upswing, but when the business cycle is nearing a plateau the profit commitments push these banks to go up the risk curve even more to hit their targets. Handelsbanken's decision to start with a risk target instead of a profit target is unusual in the

---

[47] Other banks often try to have their cake and eat it, too, by allowing risk taking in many directions but setting risk limits. In most cases this is an exercise in the seventh deadly sin as limit methodologies such as VaR (value at risk) limits rely on historical data. At the end of 2007, Merrill Lynch reported a total risk exposure of $157 million (based on a 95% confidence interval and a one-day holding period) before reporting a loss of $30 billion in 2008. Risk limits create illusions of safety.

industry. It stabilises the performance of the bank across the business cycle (an analyst at Fox Pitt Kelton once showed that Handelsbanken's profits had no correlation with GDP growth). In an industry where excessive easing and tightening of credit standards contributes to boom and bust swings, Handelsbanken even becomes a systemic stabiliser. The core assumption of Minsky's instability theory that bankers' appetite for credit risk depends on recent experience thus does not apply to Handelsbanken. The bank's decision to leave its credit policy unchanged over the cycle breaks the pattern Minsky describes:

> Acceptable financing techniques are not technologically constrained: they depend upon the subjective preferences and views of bankers and businessmen about prospects ... Success breeds a disregard of the possibility of failure; the absence of serious financial difficulties over a substantial period leads to the development of a euphoric economy in which increasing short-term financing of long positions [an example of deadly sins one and two] becomes a normal way of life.[48]

Leaving lending standards unchanged over the cycle means lending is reduced in the upswing and increased in the downturn. The bank expanded its market share after the dotcom bust. It lost significant market share from 2003 when the unsustainable credit growth started. (See Figure 6 overleaf.)

---

[48] Minsky (1986), p. 237. Also see p. 131 and pp. 198-199. One could call this the behavioural aspect of Minsky's theory.

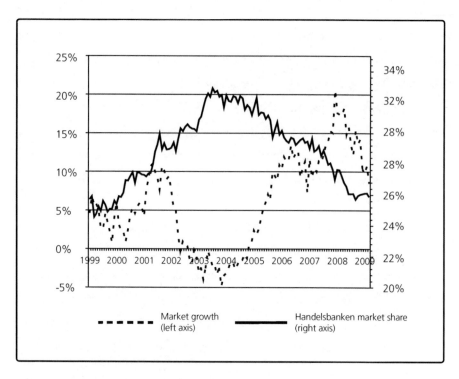

Figure 6: Swedish corporate loan growth

Unlike Minsky's bankers, Pär Boman has been increasingly cautious since my first meetings with him in 2006, i.e. during the upswing. Handelsbanken lost market share intentionally when others around them were extending ever riskier loans at historically low margins. At the end of 2008, his view was getting more positive since 'it is never easier to know who is a good credit than at the bottom of the cycle'.

Handelsbanken demonstrates that it is not an immutable fact that banks cause boom and bust patterns. Its counter-cyclical behaviour is highly desirable from the standpoint of systemic stability.

A New Paradigm for Risk Management?

Handelsbanken's concept that credit should be selected primarily by the branches and that the bank should take only risks it really understands goes against two central ideas of generally accepted bank risk management: portfolio management and diversification.

Portfolio management assumes that a loan book can be managed at an aggregate level and that one should reduce exposure to risky sectors by setting limits for the portfolio (for instance, that loans to construction companies should never be more than 10% of all loans). Diversification argues that the more heterogeneous the loan book is across countries, customer types, industries etc, the lower the overall risk since the different segments will not get into trouble at the same time.

Portfolio management

The prevailing views on this are ostensibly plausible. Yet the implicit assumption is that it is relatively easy for all players to establish what the actual riskiness of a given loan is. Arguably this is rarely the case: individual cases can be very different and many important aspects can only be evaluated by someone who knows the borrower well. For instance, is management capable, cautious, reliable? Does the borrower have a strong or weak market position? Are company owners able and willing to put in more money if needed?

As a consequence, portfolio management can be setting arbitrary limits that may not improve the loan quality at all. It may be better, as an example, to pick good customers from a bad industry, than to lend to a random sample of customers in good industries. In his book, Jan Wallander cites as evidence the fact that in the Swedish banking crisis, where loan losses came predominantly from real estate lending, the largest losses did not occur in banks with the largest share of real estate loans. What mattered was more to pick the right customers and less to get the sector allocation right. The current credit risk officer has explained that the Swedish textile industry looked terrible from a portfolio point of view – but the bank has not lost any money lending to its customers in that sector.

The loan book composition of the six main Swedish banks in 1990 is available in quite some detail (22 different borrower groups/industries), and it is worth studying. The predictive value for the amount of cumulative loan losses that each of the banks recorded in 1990-93 is virtually zero: the loan books do not differ substantially but the loan losses do. Banks that are overweight in safer sectors such as household mortgages still manage to lose a good deal more money than those that aren't.

> **" The Swedish banking crisis data suggests that there is no empirical evidence that the portfolio management of a loan book has any benefits in times of stress. "**

The Swedish banking crisis data suggests that there is no empirical evidence that the portfolio management of a loan book has any benefits in times of stress. It doesn't work when it is needed.

Diversification

Similarly, diversification founders on the cost and difficulty of evaluating credit. Information about the true credit quality of a borrower is distributed asymmetrically across potential lenders. This implies that in areas that one does not understand well the chances are that one takes on more bad assets than in one's core operations. For

Asian and European banks that held financial assets backed by US real estate this idea of adverse selection outside one's "competence zone" must sound familiar. The decision between risk management based on diversification and Handelsbanken's decentralised 'invest in what you understand better than anyone else'[49] approach ultimately rests on whether you believe that any potential lender can make an accurate assessment of a borrower's risk. Or, of course, whether such assessment is available from intermediaries such as rating agencies. It seems a mistake to ignore different levels of information in risk management – but risk management theory has largely ignored insights from pertinent areas of economics.

Information about creditworthiness is costly and difficult to obtain and as a result asymmetrically distributed between lenders. While diversification would theoretically be beneficial there are offsetting costs in the form of the 'lemon problem' as described by George Akerlof.[50] Sellers tend to have better information about the assets for sale than buyers. The market price for assets that are indistinguishable for buyers is the same. Sellers that privately know that their assets are of better than average quality will not want to sell at the market price which reflects merely average quality. So sellers will put up for sale only assets that have inferior quality. Any buyer is likely to end up with an asset that is worse than he thought – the "adverse selection" problem. In the used car market that Akerlof studied such cars are called "lemons".

---

[49] Partly because of regulatory requirements under Basel II, Handelsbanken no longer rejects quantitative methods out of hand. There is now a team of about 40 people in the credit function in Stockholm analysing the loan portfolio across the bank. Even today they are merely a complementary source of information: loan origination is still done in the branches on a customer-by-customer basis even for the very largest clients.

[50] Akerlof, George A.: "The Market for 'Lemons': Quality Uncertainty and the Market Mechanism", in: *Quarterly Journal of Economics* 84 (1970), pp. 488–500.

Diversification requires banks to acquire assets in areas outside their core expertise. Doing this, banks buy loans from banks that have better, inside information about them. Alternatively, banks diversify by making loans directly to new customer groups whose current banks have inside information about them but refuse to lend on the same terms. In the presence of information asymmetries it might be a better strategy to concentrate a bank loan book on those borrowers it knows best. Or, in the words of Mark Twain:

> Behold, the fool saith, 'Put not all thine eggs in the one basket' – which is but a manner of saying, 'Scatter your money and your attention'; but the wise man saith, 'Put all your eggs in the one basket – and *watch that basket.*'

> (Pudd'nhead Wilson's Calendar, introduction to Chapter 15 of "Pudd'nhead Wilson")

These challenges from asymmetrical information are often ignored in credit risk management. Since banks have free choice about their underwriting standards and about which assets to keep or to sell, there is an inherent risk of adverse selection. HSBC is one of the largest subprime lenders in the United States but has mostly retained loans on their balance sheet. While this book is incurring large losses it still has a better quality than the average US subprime loan. Unsurprisingly, there is widespread evidence that selling securitised subprime loans for diversification purposes has led to weaker underwriting standards.

In Akerlof's model the market breaks down unless there are remedies of the information asymmetries. Buyers know that only inferior assets are up for sale so the maximum price they are willing to pay is for the worst possible car. At this price no seller is willing to sell any more. In the second hand car market one way to remove the information asymmetries is to have an independent mechanic inspect the car.

For structured credits, unfortunately, similar attempts have not really worked. Neither credit scores for individual mortgages (e.g. FICO scores in the US) nor rating agency assessments of securitised pools of mortgages were successful in reducing the information asymmetry. Like someone who refuses to buy a used car because of the lemon problem, Handelsbanken may have been right in refusing to participate in the "pass the parcel" game of structured credit in the name of portfolio diversification. Fear of under-informed and thus adverse selection is the reason why the bank starts a new branch outside Sweden only where they can find a seasoned, experienced branch manager from that area who knows local customers very well. By having a concentrated portfolio of loans to customers they know well, the bank should, according to generally accepted risk management principles, have increased its risk exposure. In fact, the risk exposure has been lower because the concentration on customers they know well has allowed them to avoid lemons.

Handelsbanken's success in looking at the specific and the qualitative in credit analysis raises the question how much risk management can ever be a (purely) quantitative science.[51] Quantitative models could, however, already become a good deal less incorrect by dropping the heroic assumption that the true riskiness of assets is widely known.

---

[51] It is generally worrying that the conclusion for most quantitative risk analysts is that more sophisticated models are needed (e.g., *Le Monde* March 28th, 2009, "La crise expliquée par les maths", reporting from a congress of risk professionals in Paris).

8

Capital Markets Communication

Handelsbanken have an unusual style in communicating with investors and the analyst community.

No safety in numbers

The most apparent difference from other banks is that executives put enormous emphasis on not giving any guidance. Most banks give investors explicit targets they are committed to reach in the future, or at least indicate what management expect to achieve. Handelsbanken's executives sometimes sound as though they would rather have their tongue cut out than make a forward-looking statement.[52] The reason is not so much what the bank often says it is, viz. that they do not have a crystal ball for future economic development. Even if this is granted, it should still be possible within reasonable limits to indicate where the bank sees loan and deposit volumes and income going.

The real reason is twofold: to signal to the branches that there is no direction from the centre on what to do; and to avoid a situation where the bank as a whole does something stupid to meet its targets.

Resisting irrational investor pressure

Bank management also exhibits a certain positive stubbornness in resisting investor demands. Despite sometimes strong pressure from shareholders they have done what they thought was right for the bank. This includes a long list of steps they have not taken although shareholders urged them. They have accepted losing market share in

---

[52] Interestingly enough, apart from a target corridor for the bank's capital ratio the only forward-looking target I remember was a number for 30-40 new international branches in 2007, showing what degree of commitment the bank had to expansion outside Sweden.

corporate lending when risky lending started to dominate the market. They have not returned what shareholders thought was excess capital in early 2008. They have not expanded more aggressively in faster growing markets or by making acquisitions. It is well known that some investors encouraged banks that would later become the first victims of the credit crunch (HBOS, Northern Rock, Morgan Stanley) to continue their aggressive expansion which seemed to yield strong profit growth when things still went well.[53]

21st century banking – the full hundred years

Many institutions start their thought process about group strategy with capital markets expectations. For Handelsbanken these seem two separate realms and they would not take steps just because investors expect it from them. This is not to say that they do not listen: there are certainly occasions when the bank would agree with investors and thus take action. The bank listened and acted, for instance, in early 2008 when investors complained that costs were running too high, which goes against the grain of the Handelsbanken culture.

In general, however, the dialogue between the bank and its investors is similar to the dialogue between the branch and its regional bank or the chief executive: an exchange of views at the end of which those who are closest to what is really going on have to be given the freedom to do what they see as in the best interest of the bank. At a dinner in autumn 2007 an investor complained about the lacklustre performance of Handelsbanken's share price. The chief executive gave an illuminating answer: he was running the bank so it would do well over

---

[53] See *The Turner Review* (2009), pp. 45-47: 'A reasonable conclusion is that market discipline expressed via market prices cannot be expected to play a major role in constraining bank risk taking' (ibid., p. 47). Also see Augar (2009), p. 227.

the next hundred years and he would refuse to do anything that put this future at risk, even if it helped the share price or made money in the short term.

Their independence from shareholder pressure is certainly helped by having Industrivärden and Oktogonen as two large long-term shareholders. The basis, however, is a different management mindset.

Management Mindset

What characteristics of Handelsbanken's management differentiate them from most other banks? One could group them into three: the avoidance of management cult, incrementalism versus sensationalism, and long time horizons. Readers familiar with Jim Collins' management bestseller *Good to Great* will notice a number of similarities between his unsung heroes of management and the following description of Handelsbanken.

The avoidance of management cult

Investors often start a meeting flattering the egos of the people they meet: congratulating them on their achievements, as though good quarterly numbers were first and foremost the result of something the chief executive or chief financial officer had done. As an investor, I have seen this nearly always fall on fertile ground. The Handelsbanken representatives, however, rarely accept the compliment as personal.

It is difficult to find a good image but my impression is that they see themselves more as stewards than as absolute rulers.

They are not appointed, as many other executives may inwardly think, to transform the organisation by coming up with radically new and bold plans which are then executed by thousands of employees.

Rather, for Handelsbanken the bank exists and operates without anyone at the helm, and the role of executives is not to change the model but to adapt it carefully or to implement the Handelsbanken philosophy in new areas. The decision to close down proprietary trading activities in the group treasury and the capital markets division is one example, another may be the sale of its SPP insurance arm in late 2006. Pär Boman calls this process 'becoming even more Handelsbanken' (one of his colleagues called him a 'Handelsbanken fundamentalist'), and one ex-employee described it as a bank-wide development 'back to the roots'. It is no surprise that Pär Boman is the first CEO who was a branch manager.

> " Handelsbanken executives see themselves more as stewards than absolute rulers. "

In this process, even senior executives keep a fairly low profile, perhaps also because they know that given the strength of the Handelsbanken culture they would lose any fight that would pit them against the organisation and history of the bank. You will search in vain for cover stories in management magazines about Handelsbanken managers – they would probably also not be very interesting since there are no buccaneering, larger than life characters such as Sandy Weill (Citi) or Sir Fred Goodwin (RBS). How many senior executives of large banks would say that in their opinion what the branch does is more important than what they themselves do?

The idea of being a steward entails that there can be no dramatic shifts with every new chief executive. Other banks are often keen to publish major initiatives that show how much the current management is changing everything. One finds very little of this at Handelsbanken.

When they report results it is often just the bare numbers and a few illustrations of what has happened in the past quarter. Initiatives are few and far between, and they usually do not change for years whereas other banks often invent a new sensationalist initiative when the last one is becoming a bit old and boring.

Incrementalism versus sensationalism

At Handelsbanken, one of senior management's priorities is to free up time in the branches for more customer contacts. This has been very nitty-gritty work with hundreds of small changes to the routine processes, and senior management have been very involved in this important but mundane exercise. The bank values lasting, incremental improvements much more than "big bang" solutions. So unexciting, so devoid of any – positive or negative – surprises can the Handelsbanken presentations be that at one small group meeting with Pär Boman which I attended one investor actually fell asleep. Senior executives coach, nurture and push for incremental changes, and while this may be exactly the right thing for the bank it does not provide much juicy material for either the press or analysts to write about.

Long-term horizons

Being a steward allows management to think more long term. Given the continuity of the organisation they can sow the seeds for developments that will only come to fruition a long time after they have retired. Opening branches in other countries cannot make the same splash as buying a large local bank. It may take ten or fifteen years before the new branches make a substantial contribution to overall profits – starting the process now may still be the right thing to do.

9

Reaping the Benefits

What I hope to have achieved up to this point is to illustrate how Handelsbanken is run *differently* from many other large banks. It is still legitimate to ask if it is really a *better* way of running a bank. The question is relatively easy to answer for customers and employees, more difficult for shareholders.

Customers

Customers are happy with what Handelsbanken has to offer, and as a result the bank usually ranks very highly, usually as the leader among large banks, in customer satisfaction surveys such as the Swedish Svenskt Kvalitetsindex or the British EPSI Ratings. Being treated as an individual customer may help, so may the fact that there are no erratic changes of bank behaviour, for instance no sudden cut-offs of lending.

Staff

The same holds for employees: staff satisfaction surveys tend to give the bank very good ratings. Staff get good pay, responsibility and a high degree of stability. Even if this may not appeal to every banker in the City, Handelsbanken can find enough who are happy to do the job, and have the skills and experience to do it well.

Shareholders

For shareholders the question is more difficult. Undeniably Handelsbanken is in an enviable position in the current market environment post-credit crunch. The bank is gaining market share from Nordic and international banks that are forced to withdraw. It has enough capital to keep lending at rates that are much more attractive than for a long time. And it can borrow money more cheaply than the other Nordic banks because it is perceived by deposit customers and wholesale markets as prudent and low risk. Customers flock to safety so Handelsbanken is seeing faster volume growth and price increases than for many years.

But being prudent also meant missing out on phenomenal profits in good times. This was probably what Charles Prince wanted to say with his ill-timed comment about having to dance when the music was playing: if money is there to be made how can one justify to shareholders that one prefers to stand aside? Granted perhaps that other banks have a higher risk of making a loss once in a while, but could it not still be more profitable in the long run? Making lower profits than more daring banks in good times, can Handelsbanken really offset this disadvantage by benefiting from difficult times like today? Even if Handelsbanken's behaviour may be desirable for financial stability and the overall economy, is it really the better model for shareholders?

Prudence versus profits of doom

Let us compare the share price performance of Handelsbanken with that of two other large banks in Sweden, Swedbank and SEB. Unlike Handelsbanken, these two invested heavily in Eastern Europe, especially the Baltic countries, which is the main reason why their profits grew much faster.

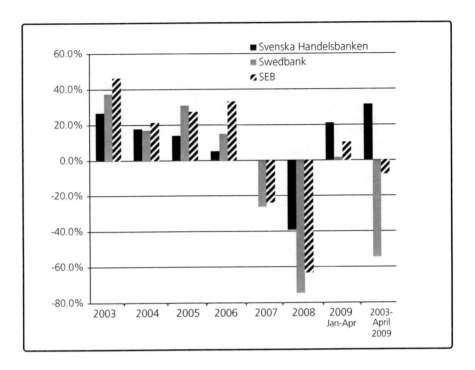

Figure 7: Long-term share price development of the three largest banks in Sweden

One can see why the disgruntled investor mentioned above was unhappy about Handelsbanken's share price performance. From 2003 to 2006, one would have made consistently more money by investing in the more aggressive banks. A fund manager buying Handelsbanken shares instead might well have been without a job at the end of 2006. Investing one hundred Swedish crowns (SEK) in Handelsbanken would have left you with 178 SEK at the end of 2006 when investing the same amount in Swedbank or SEB would have given you 241 SEK or 300 SEK, respectively. This is the deceptive phase, when imprudent behaviour appears consistently more profitable and when pressure is building even on the conservative players to relax their prudence.

But then the fortunes are turning in 2007, turning to such an extent that those who had invested their 100 SEK in Swedbank not only had to give up all their gains from the good years but also lose 55 SEK of their original investment. For shareholders, in the very long run Handelsbanken shares are probably safer *and* a better investment.

The problem for bank corporate governance, and financial stability more broadly, is that if you did not expect the financial crash you would have sold your Handelsbanken shares and would have bought Swedbank's, thus endorsing what the latter were doing. Institutional investors, who are primarily evaluated on the basis of their performance compared to the overall market, would have been under considerable pressure to explain why for years in a row they owned the "underperforming" Swedish bank. This, in essence, is why it is so difficult for investors to be a force for financial stability.

Is Handelsbanken Profit-Maximising?

Is Handelsbanken's aim to maximise profits? It does not have bonuses, cares a lot about clients and staff and is sometimes willing to forego profits. Hence it is tempting to think that it is more akin to a socialistic organisation which does not primarily aim at profits for shareholders. Nothing could be further from the truth. Jan Wallander's explicit aim was to change the bank's focus from volumes to profitability. Handelsbanken's stated goal is to have a higher return on equity than its peer group (which is what it has realised for 36 years in a row). So it is clear that profitability is Handelsbanken's dominant goal.

The bank does not, however, target a certain stock price development. While some of its Nordic peers have targets closely linked to share prices (e.g. TSR or Total Shareholder Return), Handelsbanken is agnostic about its share price, treating it with benign neglect. Unlike at many other banks, its share price development does not feature in its presentations. The underlying idea is that the bank can be held responsible for profits but that it cannot influence the share price.

Identifying management success with rising shares is even dangerous, as it invites over-promises and excessive risk-taking.

Peer group profitability

Even the statement that management is responsible for profits needs to be qualified. A bank is subject to a number of factors beyond its control – competition, interest rates, the economy at large. Therefore, Handelsbanken is careful to define its profit target in *relative* terms. Instead of aiming for an absolute level of profits or loan losses, the bank's ambition is to have a higher profitability and lower loan losses than its peers. In an unexpectedly challenging environment absolute profit targets can only be reached by going up the risk curve. Shortfalls in real operational profits are only compensated by imprudent profits from the seven deadly sins. If, like Handelsbanken, one starts with a (conservative) risk objective one cannot have absolute profit targets.

Obliquity – real profit maximisation

The most common approach in bank performance management is to cascade targets down to smaller organisational units. The idea is to set targets for them in such a way that if they all meet their targets the organisation as a whole will automatically have met its targets. So the logical step for Handelsbanken would have been as follows: if the bank wants to have a higher return on equity than its peers, then every branch should have a higher return on equity than the branches in its area.

This, however, is not how Handelsbanken works. While the bank as a whole has a long-term profitability target, the everyday behaviour of its staff is guided more by other objectives. Branch staff think about ways to increase efficiency, follow the credit policy, and strive to keep loan losses as low as possible and to serve customers well. Unlike with cascaded targets there is no mathematical certainty that following these precepts will result in superior profitability. So how do they add up to the bank-wide profit target?

The best way to explain this paradox is with a concept introduced by the economist John Kay, which he calls 'obliquity'[54]. In his words, 'obliquity is the idea that goals are often best achieved when pursued indirectly'. According to Kay, shareholder value creation or growing profits are unclear guidelines for regulating everyday decision making. Furthermore, targeting them directly opens the gates to 'get-rich-quick schemes' which, in banking, are usually variations of the seven deadly sins.

Instead, Kay argues, 'the defining purpose of business is to build good businesses'. What 'good' means can differ substantially between industries but Kay's contention is that we can tell in each individual case what makes a good company. A good airline is one that has a good safety record, does not lose bags and has minimal delays; a good supermarket is one that has nice stores in convenient locations and offers its customers competitively priced, fresh groceries while treating its suppliers well. In order to be profitable as a bank, one has to be good at banking which in turn means lending prudently, building conservative reserves and a capital cushion for challenging times, having a conservative and matched balance sheet, acting in the interest of customers and providing them with a high level of service. This is what defines a "good bank", not its profitability. These are also the precepts that Handelsbanken's branches follow in their daily activities and that are laid down in the internal publication "Our Way".

---

[54] Kay, John: The Role of Business in Society, lecture February 3rd, 1998; Kay, John: "Obliquity", in: *Financial Times*, January 17th, 2004.

Kay's idea is that if one builds a good bank then profits will follow. In this sense Handelsbanken is an exemplar of obliquity. Its consistent profitability through boom and bust periods suggests that being a good bank is a profit-maximising strategy.

Open Questions About the Success of the Handelsbanken Model

We don't know, of course, how well Handelsbanken will do in the future. The big unknown is how loan losses will compare with those of its Nordic peers. The bank has had roughly half the level of losses of its competitors for the past thirty years but it remains to be seen if this will again be the case in the current recession. The bank is certainly not immune to a global recession.

Another issue was mentioned before, in the chapter on strategy. So far the experience with international branch operations is encouraging as their branches show the same attractive profile as Swedish branches. Collectively, however, they report a significantly lower return on equity than the Swedish branch operations (about half the Swedish level). This is due to a variety of factors including the cost of branches that are still relatively young and a higher share of overhead costs in the regional branches. The branches abroad also have a more capital intensive business mix as they mostly offer corporate loans, with a lower share of other corporate products or retail banking than in Sweden. It remains to be seen whether Handelsbanken can increase the profitability to higher levels as the international branch operations mature.

Limitations of the Handelsbanken Model?

In principle, the Handelsbanken model works well for a broad range of customers, products, and geographies. The bank serves individual customers and all kinds of corporate customers, from very small ones to multinational corporations. The model is not limited to Scandinavia but works similarly well in an Anglo-Saxon country such as the UK and in continental European countries such as Poland, Germany, or the Netherlands. Handelsbanken offers not just plain vanilla commercial banking services but also cash management and trade finance services. Its asset management includes mutual funds, life insurance products, and institutional asset management services. The bank is one of the larger providers of exchange traded funds (ETFs). In investment banking, Handelsbanken covers all major product areas from foreign exchange, equity underwriting and brokerage to fixed income, commodities, and advisory services. Investment banking products such as bond underwriting and syndicated lending complement commercial banking products such as corporate loans and mortgages. As a result, Handelsbanken is one of the largest Nordic investment banks. It is the Nordic number one in commodities and structured products, number two in share trading on the Nordic stock exchanges, and among the top banks in most other areas.

So what are the areas in banking where the Handelsbanken model cannot serve as a template?

In terms of customers, it is difficult for the bank to serve very small clients. Giving customers their own relationship manager is expensive. Customers that have only very basic and limited banking needs will not generate enough income to pay for Handelsbanken's high service model.

There are few restrictions with regards to products. In general the bank offers its customers most banking products. Prudence does not rule out having substantial investment banking activities. The real limitation has more to do with risk: within each product area the bank has a low risk appetite. For instance, it offers commercial real estate financing but found most transactions in the market between 2006 and 2008 too risky and often chose not to participate. It cannot, or will not, ride the waves when finance becomes buccaneering. I don't see this as a shortcoming of the Handelsbanken model, since demand for speculative financing is arguably not a legitimate need that can be met by any type of prudent banking.

As to geographies, as already discussed a number of exotic emerging markets may not be suitable for the Handelsbanken model.

One "disadvantage" of the Handelsbanken model which the bank would freely admit is that it would find it very difficult to participate in any larger banking consolidation as either acquirer or target. The reason is largely cultural: it is hard to imagine buying another large bank with a different philosophy and then transplanting the Handelsbanken model. Likewise, anyone buying Handelsbanken would most likely dilute the model which is the bank's biggest asset.

No great limitations

To summarise, limitations with regard to customers and geographies exist but are moderate, and there are no limitations regarding products. In other words, Handelsbanken's success does not stem from operating in a small niche. Neither does it derive from the fact that most other banks operate on very different principles. It might be convenient in a crisis that competitors are more affected (although government support for weaker banks means that Handelsbanken cannot exploit this situation fully as failed competitors do not go out of business). But in good times, the banks indulging in the seven deadly sins compete for business aggressively on price as well as risk and thus present a formidable challenge to Handelsbanken as it suffers from falling market shares and shrinking margins.

The Handelsbanken model works well if other banks adhere to different strategies but it would work at least as well if more banks were to follow the Handelsbanken strategy. It values independent thinking and is not afraid to take a stance that differs from received wisdom. Consequently, there is no risk that a banking system populated with many competing Handelsbanken followers would lead to new Münchhausen markets.

Part III

Lessons Learnt

Handelsbanken was introduced to you as a good (though not necessarily the only) example of how to run a bank prudently. In this section I will address three questions. First, how much is the bank a unique case and thus of limited value for anyone else to study? Is there, for instance, anything exclusively Swedish about its model? Secondly, what exactly are the key lessons for other banks? In a more abstract way, what are the elements that make the bank a model that others might want to learn from?

And thirdly, what does our discussion up to this point imply for the ongoing debate about bank regulation? We discussed the seven deadly sins and how Handelsbanken avoids them. What does this imply for the way regulators should set goalposts and evaluate banks' business activities?

10

Is Handelsbanken Inimitable?

Even if one agrees that the Handelsbanken model is a good way of running a bank, one might doubt that others could learn anything from it. The most common objections are that the model works only in the Scandinavian market and that only a bank with Handelsbanken's history can ever hope to live by its model of banking.

At first, these objections sound plausible. Would it really be acceptable outside egalitarian Sweden that nobody earns a bonus and that the Oktogonen scheme is the same for everyone regardless of seniority? And have we not discussed at length in the chapter on strategy that Handelsbanken itself thinks not every foreign market has a suitable business culture?

Responses

Cultural compatibility is actually widespread

It is true that the Handelsbanken model may be inherently incompatible with certain markets. Yet we should not forget that the branch based model appears to work just as well in a range of countries outside Scandinavia. The bank is doing well, for instance, in an Anglo-Saxon country (Great Britain), as well as in an emerging Eastern European country (Poland). Older Handelsbanken staff in the UK have pointed out that banking there was not that different some time ago. The soil the Handelsbanken model needs consists of values such as trust, long-term relationships, caution, constancy. They can be found in many places outside Sweden, and as mentioned before there are many smaller institutions in very different countries that are similar to Handelsbanken.

Bonus motivation = bogus motivation

The question of whether you can motivate the best and brightest without bonuses should perhaps be turned around: would banking not be better without those that need high octane "heads I win, tails you lose" bonuses to do their job?

In my opinion those who have reservations about banking without bonuses are really being sceptical about motivating those who are bankers today. They might be right – but then banking might be better off without those people.

> **" Banking might be better off without those only motivated by high octane bonuses. "**

While there might not be an unlimited supply there is no shortage, either, of talented people who want to be employed yet have some entrepreneurial freedom and who want to be valued and listened to. And it would strike me as odd if they all happened to be concentrated in Sweden.

Past is prologue, but Handelsbanken is still reforming

Similarly, the second argument from history sounds plausible at first but ultimately does not withstand closer scrutiny. Jan Wallander, who played a pivotal role in shaping the Handelsbanken way from the early 1970s, admits freely that this task was long and arduous and that the bank did not change overnight. We also saw in the chapter on risk management that even today, over thirty years after Wallander started his work, there are areas where the Handelsbanken ideas still have to be fully implemented. Yet I would argue that far from proving that the task is impossible, this shows that very different organisations can indeed transform themselves. Few of the tasks involved are particularly easy or quick. Becoming more like Handelsbanken may not increase the next quarterly profit. But from Wallander's experience it seems that it is feasible and worthwhile for bank executives who want their organisation to survive and prosper for the next hundred years. There is nothing from his experience in the 1970s either to suggest that adopting the model has large initial costs.

Can We Afford Not to Learn from Them?

A bank becoming more like Handelsbanken will, of course, lose some people and some profit streams. Yet is it really worth keeping them if the people are there only for large bonuses from risky undertakings for which the bank bears the risk? Is there really any value creation for shareholders in making profits from taking speculative bets on market risk? The real cost of turning into a more prudent institution may be more in the perception of shareholders than real – the insight from the previous chapter. If investors reward imprudent risk-taking as long as it earns handsome profits, one will certainly upset them by "de-risking" the bank and concentrating on core franchise activities only. However one will not be upsetting them when one's profits do not, like everyone else's, disintegrate.

And can we afford not to learn from them *now*?

Arguably, given the above, the aftermath of the financial crisis could be the one and only time to do it. For bank executives, the current risk averse investor sentiment may be the once-in-a-lifetime opportunity to implement this genuine blueprint for better banking.

11

Implications for Other Banks

Being a basic, simple "utility" bank can be remarkably difficult. A number of banks that could have laid claim to the title were badly bruised in the credit crunch. Unfortunately, being prudent in some areas but not all does not amount to much prudence overall. As banks are fragile creatures it takes just one of the seven deadly sins to backfire to bring the entire bank into difficulties. In addition, many of the elements in the Handelsbanken model are interconnected and would not work in isolation.

The description of Handelsbanken contains many elements that other banks might find useful to copy. But while the Handelsbanken is one proven model for prudent banking there might be others. Hence, we will now discuss several more abstract lessons from the Handelsbanken case study that apply to all types of prudent banking.

Business Model

We started by discussing Handelsbanken's different approach to strategy. A key lesson was how important it is for a bank to have a distinct business model. This has necessarily to do with what a bank is good at, or rather better at than its competitors. It leads inevitably to decisions about what it is not good at and what it will hence avoid doing. In my job as a consultant and as an investment professional I have got to know most of the larger banks in Europe and their management: in very few cases was there a real business model. Banks differ by what they do – which customers they serve, in which regions, with which products. But there is rarely a unique system or approach – a business model, in short. Strategy for most banks is equal to portfolio choices, not to a firm-specific business model.

The portfolio approach to strategy assumes that the dynamics of a given market exist prior to and independently of those who decide to participate in it. Banks, in other words, are market takers. Unsurprisingly, when things go wrong portfolio players find many factors outside their control. They put the correct weighting of different portfolio parts ahead of selecting good customers. They are happy taking their representative share of good markets without knowing that taking a representative share of a market means being coupled to its ups and downs.

Handelsbanken's customer picking is not immune to sector trends, but the link is much weaker. You can have a regional manager rejoicing about having more than 25% market share in corporate loans but less than 10% of corporate bankruptcies. And since you do what you are good at, and not just go where the money is, you know much more what to do once the going gets tough.

Ask Handelsbanken's competitor Swedbank, which made a lot of money in the Baltic countries during the good years, how much they are in charge in the macroeconomic upheaval in these countries and how much they can decouple themselves from these developments beyond their control. Or ask competitors DnB Nor and Nordea about their substantial lending to the shipping sector, an industry that is very cyclical. Did any of them really have a competitive advantage compared to their competition? Is it a business where they are in control of their own destiny? Doing business in markets because they are profitable and growing is a nice thing in good times. But doing business only in areas that you are very good at gives added protection during bad times. Bank strategists may be better advised to start with an honest assessment of competences before looking for areas to deploy them. Looking for the juiciest markets so often leads banks to enter at the top of the market and to become the victim of adverse selection when more competent competitors retrench.

Motivation Processes

Another chapter in the Handelsbanken rule book from which others may want to borrow pertains to human resources. Many banks' staff incentives induce excessive risk-taking, as has been noted. If things go well and there is a profit, the banker responsible gets a large bonus. That is, in good times a substantial share of profits goes to staff rather than shareholders. Large investment banks often pay between half and two-thirds of revenues to their staff. If, on the other hand, things go wrong, shareholders bear the loss. The banker may lose his or her job but it is not unusual that the bank has to retain them to manage the positions that have incurred large losses. This is what happened at AIG, the US insurance company that was sunk by credit derivative trades. It decided to retain the traders responsible for the losses – and even pay them bonuses – because they were the only ones who knew those positions well enough to "manage them down". Such a bonus culture is not the only cause of imprudent banking but it creates strong incentives to indulge in the seven deadly sins.

The basis for staff recruitment and retention at Handelsbanken, on the other hand, is a fixed salary in line with or slightly above market level, paired with intrinsic motivation. As described, this comes from having a large degree of entrepreneurial freedom at the branch level. While entrepreneurial freedom is the non-monetary carrot, the non-monetary stick is internal competition. Comparing performance with similar units every month is like a friendly but serious competition that leaves little scope for complacency.

As most banks are aware that they must change their compensation model, Handelsbanken may be a good example of how to make compensation models less risky without inviting complacency. If staff satisfaction surveys are anything to go by, employees might even welcome such a change.

Organisational Structure and Culture

Another interesting recipe is Handelsbanken's simple structure, which has remained largely unchanged for decades, and in which people stay in the same or similar roles for a long time. It allows a strong shared culture to develop since everyone can see that most other parts of the company operate similarly. Furthermore, people know what they have to do and what others do, which makes co-operation easier than in an organisation where roles and structures constantly shift.

It is also a way to keep the institutional memory – what has and has not worked in similar situations in the past – alive for much longer. It activates a bank's history, and having a strong shared sense of history in turn promotes cohesion.

And lastly, banks might benefit from moving away from planning and budgeting towards more of the peripatetic management style where managers meet with those reporting to them mostly for exchange of ideas.

Nobody has any reason to do silly things to hit their numbers, nor does anybody have a reason to be defensive. Meetings between line manager and direct report become more of a joint problem-solving effort.

Supervision

One major reason for the occurence of the seven deadly sins is the fact that they are not reported properly and often appear indistinguishable from prudent activities.

In addition, branch autonomy requires very good supervision tools. Other banks might hence find it useful to develop more meaningful controlling instruments and to fine-tune them constantly. Making risks transparent and reporting the profit contribution of the seven deadly sins separately might go a long way to reducing their attraction.

Attitude

What might be most difficult to change is cultural attitude. It will not be easy to turn executives from omnipresent decision-makers into coaches who help their subordinates without steering their decisions. It will be terribly difficult to resist the temptation of easy, imprudent profits and to withstand the pressure from shareholders.

Establishing a culture similar to Handelsbanken's involves reprogramming an organisation's values from a primacy of growth

> **"** A culture of stability, low costs and occasional contrarianism needs to be imitated. **"**

to one of stability, from profit increases to low credit and operating costs, and from riding the trend of the day to being, at times, contrarian.

Original Thinking About Risks

In risk management, one key insight from Handelsbanken is that although quantitative models can be instructive they are often misleading in important regards. Many relevant factors are very, very case specific and qualitative. History, on which quantitative models rely, may not repeat itself; many scenarios that have never happened before are conceivable.

And most importantly, the question "what are we really good at?" should be asked in debates about risk management just as much as in those about strategy. Many types of risk may simply not be worth taking because one is no better than anyone else. One may actually be worse than others and hence end up holding all the wrong cards.

If a bank does not have any "edge" in understanding the US housing market, it should not own any securities based on US mortgages, diversification or not. While these securities may earn a higher income than government securities, they do not have a legitimate place in such a bank's liquidity portfolio. Similarly, if there is no reason to believe that a bank is better at forecasting interest rates it should not implicitly speculate by borrowing short and lending long. There is very rarely a case for banks to run a mismatched balance sheet. That is not to deny that taking risks where one does not have an advantage will often produce several years of profits. But these profits are not of the same quality as profits from core customer operations. They have a high probability of turning into losses that can eventually wipe out all the cumulative profits.

Handelsbanken's Habitat

It was mentioned above that Handelsbanken can come across as a slightly "socialist bank". It lacks bonuses, and values staff and customer satisfaction highly. In addition, it has never participated in capitalist endeavours such as large M&A activity. Ironically, it is probably more capitalist than its peers, which required government support and would have gone under in a truly capitalist, Schumpeterian "creative destruction". Handelsbanken, on the other hand, never needed any state support.

Countercyclical, crisis ready – not driving towards crisis

Pär Boman expressed the view that the bank has for a long time been run on the basis that if there is a complete collapse of the global financial system, Handelsbanken will be the last organisation left standing. When such a meltdown appeared possible after the Lehman failure in September 2008, Handelsbanken supported government intervention. Nevertheless, ongoing state support for other banks represents a substantial competitive advantage against Handelsbanken. For instance, government guarantee schemes for banks' debt issuance allow those institutions to raise funds at costs that are usually below market rates. In many cases, without government guarantees those banks could not raise funds at all and would follow in Lehman's footsteps. Handelsbanken would clearly benefit if one of its competitors disappeared. But instead of letting Schumpeterian capitalism run its course, governments have propped up its "victims". Imprudent banks have been chastened but their imprudent banking operations survive thanks to a protective government holding its umbrella over them.

My concern in this regard is different from the argument that shareholders in financial institutions will have a high risk appetite as they know governments will bail them out. I don't find this moral hazard argument convincing. Shareholders have incurred large losses even where the bail-out has not wiped out their equity entirely, and there is no evidence that at the time of writing shareholders have an excessive appetite for financial risk. Yet, as the discussion on the reasons for the seven deadly sins shows, shareholders were only one, probably not even the main, reason for imprudence in banking operations. Shareholders have in most cases been severely

> **If the seven deadly sins are not eradicated, government intervention will have averted imminent disaster at a high cost.**

punished but government intervention has ensured that financial institutions survive intact. That leaves most of the drivers behind the seven deadly sins in place. There will still be the temptation to indulge in them because doing so will create revenues indistinguishable from prudent income sources. There will still be peer pressure, vainglorious bankers and the temptation to ride the waves. In addition, in most banks there are still the same people whose habits were formed over decades when the seven deadly sins were lucrative and widely applauded.

If the seven deadly sins are not eradicated, government intervention will have averted imminent disaster at a high cost: ensuring the survival of imprudent banks and putting prudent banking operations at a relative disadvantage to them.

12

Implications for Bank Regulation

The point about the seven deadly sins of imprudent banking is that there is no single cause behind the cataclysmic institutional failures in the credit crunch. Investment banks, commercial banks, insurance companies and building societies all incurred large losses, for different reasons. But they all suffered from imprudent banking of one sort or another. Some benefited from the maturity mismatches of their balance sheet, others from high-yielding non-core assets or from dealing with the shadow banking system in the form of SIVs and conduits. Imprudent profits for another group of institutions came from emerging markets, real estate banking, or from lending to financially overstretched individuals and companies.

As imprudent banking can look innocuous and profitable for many consecutive years, many companies could not resist the temptation to "dance while the music was playing" and became victims when the music stopped.

They got away with this deterioration of earnings quality because in financial statements prudent and imprudent activities look alike. Unfortunately, changes that are presented as silver bullets, such as the separation of commercial and investment banking or a reform of banking bonuses, will at best solve a small part of the problem and may even have unintended consequences.

In my view the Handelsbanken case suggests three regulatory priorities:

1) A more meaningful separation of prudent and imprudent activities in financial statements.

2) A more "detective" mindset in people supervising banks.

3) A stricter institutional separation of those institutions that in return for some form of government guarantee renounce the seven deadly sins, and those that won't.

More Meaningful Reporting

Financial reporting is not to blame for being "pro-cyclical". It is to blame for its failure to distinguish prudent, safe income streams from risky, imprudent ones. The balance sheet of a bank that lends low amounts in local currency to solid customers looks identical to one that lends too much, in yen or Swiss francs, to over-indebted borrowers. Bringing the seven deadly sins into the daylight of public scrutiny must be a major priority for accounting standards boards.

This must entail reporting on the average balance sheet mismatches and the resulting higher income compared to a perfectly matched balance sheet. Institutions should also explain how they calculate internal treasury pricing.

> **❝ Bringing the seven deadly sins into the daylight of public scrutiny must be a major priority for accounting standards boards. ❞**

More disclosure is required on the financial situation of borrowers. Financial statements should include information about their balance sheet mismatches and the affordability of their loans. Product level information about teaser prices and price resets would be highly desirable.

Investors need greater transparency on dealings with the shadow banking system, including economic interests and the worst case contingent liabilities. This should also include disclosure about the income generated from these activities.

To achieve greater transparency on non-core assets an institution should describe the assets it has not originated itself in its core business. The institution should also disclose the associated income and describe the rationale for holding these assets (e.g. principal investment, liquidity portfolio, repossessed assets, trading assets).

A New Regulatory Mindset

Until they have succeeded, regulators will have to look past financial statements and ratios to the substance of operations. They need to understand the nature of a bank's business to sniff out examples of the seven deadly sins. In banking and finance there are many ways to sin, and the weak sinners will always find new ways to return to their wrongful ways, avoiding any new explicit rule. In this regard nothing much has changed since some Catholics in the 17th century complied with the ban on eating meat on Fridays by declaring beaver to be fish. Banks reclassify assets between the banking book and the trading book, and regulators that do not look at the substance of what is going on are bound to give their subjects a clean bill of health. As regulators themselves discover, regulation based on rules and ratios alone does not work.[55]

---

[55] See IMF (April 2009), chapter three "Detecting Systemic Risks".

Regulators may find it useful to ask "cui bono?" and follow the incentives of different players to find imprudent behaviour. Very often it is not so much greed as sheer pressure on core operations which leads financial institutions to try to gamble their way out of a dilemma. The US Savings and Loans crisis had its roots in margin pressure from disintermediation (money market funds offering better interest rates than bank deposits) that led many of them to increase interest rate risk-taking. In environments of low yields, pension funds and insurances that have to pay largely fixed guaranteed rates are under pressure to go up the risk curve in search of higher income. In Eastern Europe, competitive pressure and falling margins led banks to offer ever riskier loans and to expand into riskier geographies.

Wages of sin is false profit

In each of these cases understanding the motivation of financial institutions is very informative since indulging in the seven deadly sins to create new profits becomes much more likely when core operations are under pressure. Perhaps it is no coincidence that some banking markets with a stable oligopolistic structure and limited competitive pressure (e.g. France, Italy, Canada) have weathered the financial crisis better than markets with intense competition and many new entrants (US, UK, Germany, Eastern Europe).

Resilient ratios

As imprudent activities may work for some time, all financial ratios that regulators look at will necessarily look strong during good times. But financial stability does not consist in strong ratios but in having ratios that will still be resilient under difficult scenarios. We have already noted (see the section starting on page 49) that financial ratios were worse than useless in identifying financial institutions which subsequently required government intervention.

Under the Basel II framework for bank capital adequacy, regulators should check each individual entity they supervise under a stress scenario. On the basis of our insights on risk management – good risk management should plan for all conceivable future scenarios, not for a rerun of historical data – this approach is sensible.

It has obviously worked much less well in practice as regulators failed to anticipate capital requirements and are still catching up. The extremely undesirable effect for economies all around the world is that just when banks incur large losses and have less capital to lend, regulators expect them to have more capital for the same amount of assets. This further restricts the appetite of banks for any new asset, regardless of its profitability.

Raising the bar on capital requirements for all banks seems a fairly crude approach. It would be desirable to penalise only those banks that are active in risky or even imprudent business areas and could hence face a sharp fall in capital ratios. Higher capital requirements across the board might even create new pressure on banks – see the "cui bono?" examples above – to find wondrous sources of profits when return on equity in their core operations becomes depressed.

Hercule Poirot not Hercule Penpusher needed

The reasons for the stark failure of regulatory stress testing are seemingly elusive. My supposition would be, though, that it was a mix of looking too much at form rather than substance, relying too much on quantitative models (e.g. value at risk for trading book assets) despite knowing they are flawed, and putting too much trust in banks' own models. In other words, the regulators acted more like financial analysts when they should have been detectives. As financial disclosure is insufficient to detect the seven deadly sins, regulators need to ask the banks they supervise a lot of additional questions. Basel II stress testing allows them to ask for as much information as they want but apparently this was not used enough. For instance, in the absence of any information about a bank's customers it is impossible to rule out customer balance sheet mismatches or over-indebtedness, the second and third of the deadly sins. Therefore, 'the authorities must look through the veil of the bank's balance sheet to the balance sheets of the organisations that the bank finances'.[56]

Regulatory application, not escalation

If one accepts that stress testing under Basel II is a powerful tool that was not used properly by most regulators, current regulatory priorities are worrying.

Regulators are in favour of new responsibilities such as macro-prudential regulation or the closer inspection of systemic connectedness of financial institutions. I am not aware of any institution that was prudently managed itself but ran intro trouble because of macro developments or events at other financial institutions.

Each problem case could have been identified in isolation had one but looked for the seven deadly sins. The responsibilities regulators want to add to their mandate do not appear strictly necessary. In addition, it is unclear why regulators who have failed in their traditional job – spotting risks at individual institutions – should be any better at the much more difficult task of spotting risks that only exist at a higher, systemic level. If supervising a single institution is complex then surely supervising the entire financial system, a web of all financial institutions, is more complex still.

---

[56] Minsky (1986), p. 361.

Some of the new regulatory ideas might even have counterproductive unintended consequences. For instance, one popular idea of regulators who place a high importance on the connectedness of financial institutions is to charge an additional capital levy on large institutions that are closely connected to the rest of the system and thus too big to fail. There could be no better incentive for these banks to avoid this penalty by pushing as many activities as possible into the shadow banking system.

Instead of this regulatory creep a better priority might be to discharge their core job of stress testing individual institutions more diligently and intelligently.

Anticipating bail-outs must stop

Banks have not got their scenario thinking particularly right either. We saw earlier (Figure 3) that of the top 25 European banks only three (Handelsbanken, Deutsche Bank, BBVA) went into the financial crisis sufficiently prepared and did not have to raise more capital and/or apply for state support. Relying on quantitative modelling was never likely to get things right, especially as it is blind to conceivable scenarios that have simply not happened in the past which quantitative data cover. But Andrew Haldane of the Bank of England offers an additional interesting account of the reasons why banks' stress tests failed:

> A few years ago, ahead of the present crisis, the Bank of England and the FSA commenced a series of seminars with financial firms, exploring their stress-testing practices. The first meeting of that group sticks in my mind. We had asked firms to tell us the sorts of stress which they routinely used for their stress-tests. A quick survey suggested these were very modest stresses. We asked why. Perhaps disaster myopia – disappointing, but perhaps unsurprising? Or network externalities – we

understood how difficult these were to capture? No. There was a much simpler explanation according to one of those present. There was absolutely no incentive for individuals or teams to run severe stress tests and show these to management. First, because if there were such a severe shock, they would very likely lose their bonus and possibly their job. Second, because in that event the authorities would have to step-in anyway to save a bank and others suffering a similar plight. All of the other assembled bankers began subjecting their shoes to intense scrutiny. The unspoken words had been spoken. The officials in the room were aghast. Did banks not understand that the official sector would not underwrite banks mis-managing their risks? Yet history now tells us that the unnamed banker was spot-on. His was a brilliant articulation of the internal and external incentive problem within banks. When the big one came, his bonus went and the government duly rode to the rescue.[57]

More recently, the Bank and FSA have been engaged in some practical work with banks, running stress tests through their models on common scenarios. When asked to assess the consequences of a macro stress-test, the like of which we are currently experiencing, some banks have found it problematic.

In defence, they have suggested that such an exercise was only conducted annually as part of their Basel II preparations and as such new stress tests would take months to conduct. This too was revealing.

If even the most obvious stress-test took many weeks to prepare and assess, how could these tests meaningfully be used to manage risk? The short answer, I think, is that stress-testing was not being meaningfully used to manage risk. Rather, it was being used to manage regulation. Stress-testing was not so much regulatory arbitrage as regulatory camouflage.

---

[57] Haldane (2009), pp. 6-7

As a consequence, regulators will have to play a much larger role. For the purpose of (Basel pillar II) stress testing, instead of using historical data to run a bank through many different shades of the recent past, they will have to think more creatively about all the things that could go wrong and all the scenarios that would present a problem even if they have not happened before.

Their job might become more similar to that of commercial lawyers, who have to anticipate all eventualities in order to make watertight contracts. In the same way regulators may have to think creatively about the worst conceivable situations for a bank and ensure that the bank takes adequate measures against them. And they will have to do their own modelling based on economic substance rather than meagre bits of accounting information that group together the prudent and the imprudent.

Isolating Imprudent Banking: a Better Alternative to a New Glass-Steagall Act

You will have guessed that I am sceptical about the separation of commercial and investment banking by means of a new Glass-Steagall Act. Too many pure commercial banks have had massive balance sheet problems of their own. The argument for a separation is that "utility banks" could no longer engage in "risky trading activities". But we have discussed before that a large number of problems for banks came from other areas that would still be present in the so-called utility banks. After all, a large number of classic retail banks with no investment banking suffered large losses from toxic assets in their liquidity portfolio as part of their treasury operations and not as part of proprietary trading (Bradford & Bingley, Alliance & Leicester, Deutsche Postbank, to name but a few). An even larger range of basic commercial banks are discovering big problems from imprudent lending in their banking book. Liquidity problems affected pure commercial banks such as Northern Rock.

On the other hand, some investment banking flow businesses – offering foreign exchange or interest rate products to corporate customers or underwriting their corporate bonds – are useful to clients, low risk for the banks, but would be ruled out under a revived Glass-Steagall act.[58] Handelsbanken represents a good example of a combination of commercial and investment banking that is beneficial to customers and of low risk for shareholders.

As mentioned, Martin Wolf, who introduced the terms "utility banking" and "casino banking", has not defined them precisely. It is not clear, for instance, if lending would be an activity of the utility bank or the casino bank. On the one hand, the transformation of deposits into loans with a longer maturity is an essential function for the economy so lending should be part of the utility bank. On the other hand, lending is risky and can be done imprudently so it could arguably also belong to the casino bank. This, however, would lead to the unacceptable situation where the government has to bail out a casino bank if the alternative would be to starve the economy of credit. This shows that separating utility and casino activities is not enough. It is necessary to tell the utility bank not just what it can do but also how it can do it.

Hence a better regulatory move might be to limit explicit deposit insurance and implicit state guarantee for all liabilities to those institutions that commit to:

---

[58] This is the reason why Minsky opposes Glass-Steagall and the separation of commercial and investment banking: 'restrictions on banks acting as dealers, underwriters, and financial advisers are unwarranted legacies of the 1930s.' (Minsky 1986, p. 355).

1) Owning only a very limited amount of non-core assets. Apart from customer assets (loans), banks should hold securities only for the purpose of being liquid and not for making profits, so non-customer assets could be limited to very safe securities such as government bonds. This rule would disallow the holding of "toxic assets", and it would rule out proprietary, speculative trading while allowing banks to offer their customers sensible investment banking services as a flow business with low risks to the bank. A similar rule would apply to off-balance sheet positions such as derivatives. They could be used to reduce risks (hedging positions and matching assets and liabilities more closely) but qualifying institutions could not engage in other derivatives operations in order to generate profits.

2) Keeping their own balance sheets as closely matched as possible or incurring punitive capital requirements for mismatches.

3) Becoming subject to greater product-level regulation that would suppress balance sheet mismatches at the borrower level or generally lending to companies or individuals that cannot afford the loan. It could also be used to restrain banks from making loans that are de facto equity or, in Minsky's terminology, "Ponzi finance" (PIK loans, mezzanine loans).[59]

---

[59] Minsky distinguishes three types of financing. Hedge financing is structured such that the borrower can repay interest and principal of his debt from his operating cash flows. With speculative financing the borrower's operating cash flows are sufficient to service but not to repay his debt. It is riskier than hedge financing because of the risk that the debt cannot be rolled over. In Ponzi financing structures, new debt is needed both to service and to repay existing debt. Pay in kind (PIK) loans (common in leveraged finance) let the borrower pay interest in additional loans. They are thus a form of Ponzi financing.

4) Regulators performing more substantive stress tests around conceivable scenarios as discussed above, implying much greater capital requirements for potentially imprudent activities such as emerging market banking or cyclical real estate lending, etc.

5) Reforming their pay structures, ideally abolishing bonuses altogether in the way that Handelsbanken has done, in order to eliminate incentives to find regulatory loopholes, and to discourage engaging in the seven deadly sins again.

6) Limiting their counterparty exposure to other institutions that commit to the same standards and that would be bailed out. This rule would take care of the "Lehman risk" that many regulators are concerned about, i.e. that prudently managed institutions could be bankrupted because one of their counterparties defaults.

These guidelines would define more closely the concept of a "utility bank" that does not, or cannot, engage in significant "casino" operations. Institutions that would not commit to these requirements for deposit guarantees would be free to trade on their own account and deal with specialist customers but would forfeit any state guarantee.

The last rule stipulates that utility banks could not do any business with casino banks. This would greatly reduce the systemic risk of letting a casino institution fail. Nevertheless, regulators still need to create a credible framework to let failed casino operations go bankrupt.

Epilogue

Current Bad Practice is Avoidable

The seven deadly sins are the transmission mechanism between certain macroeconomic conditions and boom/bust cycles in the financial industry.

Financial crises can only happen when enough banks have succumbed and engaged in business activities that are neither sound nor prudent.

The Handelsbanken example shows that it is by no means unavoidable that banks act imprudently. It also refutes a number of popular theories. It is often claimed that only a bank that is small, or privately owned by its management, or stays well clear of investment banking, can avoid becoming a systemic risk. In addition, it is often assumed that banks are too optimistic in booms and too pessimistic in busts so that their behaviour acts as a "shock amplifier". However, Handelsbanken is a large bank with substantial investment banking operations and is quoted on the stock exchange, and yet it is stable and even acts as a shock absorber for the banking system.

Just as many different institutions fell for the seven deadly sins and ended up as victims of the financial crisis, many different institutions can be run prudently. It all depends on how they are managed.

Better Banking Already Exists and Works

By describing the main aspects of Handelsbanken's management model we have shown what prudent, risk avoiding banking practices can look like. I think it is warranted to call this a blueprint for better banking. It is a strategy that is profit maximising over a long time-horizon – including financial crises. At the same time, because of its unchanging credit policy it avoids contributing to destabilising boom and bust cycles on the industry level.

Handelsbanken does not have the copyright on prudent banking. I am sure that there are several smaller banks in different countries that operate on similar principles. Compared to them Handelsbanken has the advantage, as an interesting model for others, that it is large and active in many different markets. Moreover, it has had nearly four decades of continuity with "the Handelsbanken way", during which management have tweaked, refined and perfected the model.

It Can Be Judiciously Imitated

It would not be advisable to copy Handelsbanken's rule book slavishly. Insights need to be adapted, adjusted to circumstances. Handelsbanken's adoption of internet banking – a website for each branch – is a good illustration of this art of adaptation. The process involves taking into account the interconnections between the different elements, and a pick-and-mix approach will be difficult. To take just one example, the remuneration model that foregoes bonuses works only if staff are intrinsically motivated by entrepreneurial freedom, and if they are confident in the organisational structure. Equally, branch autonomy requires a strong controlling system and culture, and local decision-making authority requires a high level of competence.

So the bad news is that it is not a model that can be adopted overnight. The change in culture and mentality will take years, or even decades. Or it might even never be finished: after all, part of the Handelsbanken ethos is to continue thinking about further ways to make the bank more "Handelsbanken". Its mindset is similar to *kaizen*, continuous improvement, the Japanese production philosophy which is now applied throughout the world. And adopting a similar spirit is unlikely to please everyone. After all, there are many who have benefited individually from the seven deadly sins.

The good news is that implementing a similar model at other banks is very likely to be the right decision long term. It will render a bank simpler and more manageable. It will reduce the risks for the individual bank and make it a shock absorber, not a shock amplifier, for the financial system.

It is likely to leave all stakeholders better off, with the exception of those that could cash in on profits from the seven deadly sins during the good times; and their grief would be tolerable.

Regulators Can and Must Learn From it Too

Following financial disaster in the past, politicians have changed the structure and supervision of financial markets in efforts to eradicate sources of instability. In the US, in 1913, the establishment of the Federal Reserve Banking system as lender of last resort followed the 1907 banking crisis, and after the Great Depression the Roosevelt administration made fundamental changes to the fabric of financial markets with the SEC (securities regulator), the FDIC (deposit insurance), the Glass-Steagall Act and the Federal Home Loan system. While not all of it has been perfect it has greatly reduced some financial destabilisers. In the US, securities lending on 10% margin and bank runs have not happened again.

Few such changes have been made in response to banking crises in the more recent decades, often with the effect that the seven deadly sins have repeatedly caused new crises.

We touched on some desirable changes that would reduce the appeal of the seven deadly sins. One would be to distinguish in banks' financial statements between profits from prudent banking and others. Another would be to grant an essential privilege such as deposit insurance only to banks that renounce the seven deadly sins.

Regulation will have to differentiate more between financial institutions – based on their management practices. Handelsbanken's risk profile is quite unlike that of most of its peers, although they all operate in similar markets. Applying the same rules across the board does not make sense and even runs the risk of rewarding the riskiest practices. In order to differentiate more between management practices, regulators will have to go beyond looking at financial ratios. They will generally have to become more intrusive, more immersed in the details of the companies they supervise.

> **" We should learn from Handelsbanken's example, overhaul the structure and institutions of financial markets and contain the seven deadly sins. "**

Unlike most other banks Handelsbanken has single-handedly come up with a management system to avoid the temptation of the seven deadly sins. The Handelsbanken way is the wax in the ears of those that know that sailing on financial seas one is likely to encounter sirens promising quick profits. They have thus demonstrated that banking does not have to be a cycle of financial euphoria ending in a massive hangover.

Governments and regulators should learn from Handelsbanken's example, overhaul the structure and institutions of financial markets and thus expunge, or at least contain, the seven deadly sins.

Bibliography

Augar, Philip: *Chasing Alpha: How Reckless Growth and Unchecked Ambition Ruined the City's Golden Decade*, London 2009.

Bank of International Settlement (ed.): *Bank Failures in Mature Economies, BIS Working Paper 13*, 2004.

Brunnige, Olof: *Using History in Organizations: How Managers Make Purposeful Reference to History in Strategy Processes*, in: *Journal of Organizational Change Management* 22, 2009, pp. 8-26.

Cable, Vince: *The Storm, The World Economic Crisis & What It Means*, London 2009.

Caprio, Gerard Jr., and Daniela Klingebiel: *Bank Insolvency: Bad Luck, Bad Policy or Bad Banking?*, paper presented at the Annual Bank Conference on Development Economics 1996.

Chancellor, Edward: *Devil Take the Hindmost, A History of Financial Speculation*, New York 1999.

Cohan, William D.: *House of Cards: a Tale of Hubris and Wretched Excess on Wall Street*, New York 2009.

Collins, Jim: *Good to Great, Why Some Companies Make the Leap and Others Don't*, London 2001.

Cooper, George: *The Origin of Financial Crises, Central Banks, Credit Bubbles and the Efficient Market Fallacy*, Petersfield 2008.

Ferguson, Niall: *The Pity of War*, London 1998.

Galbraith, John Kenneth: *A Short History of Financial Euphoria*, New York/London 1994.

Haldane, Andrew G.: *Why Banks Failed the Stress Test*, in: BIS Review 18, 2009, pp. 1-14.

Hildebrand, Karl-Gustaf: *Banking in a Growing Economy, Svenska Handelsbanken since 1871*, translated by D. Simon Harper, Stockholm 1971.

International Monetary Fund: *The Recent Financial Turmoil – Initial Assessment, Policy Lessons, and Implications for Fund Surveillance*, April 2009.

International Monetary Fund: *Lessons of the Financial Crisis for Future Regulation of Financial Institutions and Markets and for Liquidity Management*, February 2009.

Juglar, François Clément: *Des crises commerciales et de leur retour périodique en France, en Angleterre et aux Etats-Unis*, Paris 1862.

Keynes, John Maynard: *The General Theory of Employment*, in: *Quarterly Journal of Economics* 51, 1937, pp. 209-223.

Kindleberger, Charles P.: *Manias, Panics, and Crashes, A History of Financial Crises*, New York 2000.[60]

Laeven, Luc, and Valencia Fabian: *Systemic Banking Crises – a New Database*, IMF Working Paper November 2008.

Lazear, Edward P., and Sherwin Rosen: *Rank-Order Tournaments as Optimum Labor Contracts, Journal of Political Economy* 89, 1981, pp. 841-64.

Lindgren, Håkan, Gustav Sjöberg, and Jan Wallander: *Bankkrisen*, Stockholm 1994.

---

[60] I hope to be forgiven for having footnotes also in the bibliography but this charming book contains a description of 19th century events that sounds very familiar today: 'As invariably happens in serious commercial crises [1879], loud voices were raised demanding the intervention of the public authorities. [...] The Riksdag [the Swedish parliament] [...] at the very moment when the crisis reached its height, became under these circumstances the scene of the most vigorous efforts to evoke measures conducive to the benefit of the business world.' (p. 55) Plus ça change.

Lindsay, R. Murray, and Theresa Libby: *Svenska Handelsbanken: Controlling a Radically Decentralized Organization without Budgets*, in: *Accounting Education* 22, 2007, pp. 625-640.

Mackay, Charles: *Memoirs of Extraordinary Popular Delusions and the Madness of Crowds*, London 1841.

Minsky, Hyman P.: *Can "It" Happen Again? Essays on Instability and Finance*, New York 1982.

Minsky, Hyman P.: *Stabilizing an Unstable Economy*, New Haven and London 1986.

Minsky, Hyman P.: *Reconstituting the United States' Financial Structure: Some Fundamental Issues*, Institute of European Finance Research Paper 16 (1992).

Nakaso, Hiroshi: *The Financial Crisis in Japan During the 1990s: How the Bank of Japan Responded and the Lessons Learnt*, Bank of International Settlement (BIS) Working Papers 6, 2001.

Shiller, Robert: *The Subprime Solution*, Princeton/Oxford 2008.

Shiller, Robert J.: *Irrational Exuberance*, Princeton 2005.

Shiller, Robert: *Bubbles, Human Judgement, and Expert Opinion*. Cowles Foundation Discussion Paper 1303, 2001.

Shull, Bernard: *The Limits of Prudential Supervision: Experience in the United States*, in: *Economic Notes* 3, 1995, pp. 585-612.

Soros, George: *The New Paradigm for Financial Markets: The Credit Crisis of 2008 and What It Means*, New York 2008.

Svenska Handelsbanken 1871-1921, A Retrospective, Stockholm 1921.

Taleb, Nassim Nicholas: *The Black Swan: The Impact of the Highly Improbable*, London 2007.

Taylor, John B.: *Getting Off Track, How Government Actions and Interventions Caused, Prolonged, and Worsened the Financial Crisis*, Stanford 2009.

Taylor, John B.: *The Financial Crisis and the Policy Responses: An Empirical Analysis of What Went Wrong*, keynote speech at the Bank of Canada, November 2008.

Turner, Adair: *The Financial Crisis and the Future of Financial Regulation*, speech on January 21st, 2009.

The Turner Review, A Regulatory Response to the Global Banking Crisis, FSA report March 2009.

Wallander, Jan: *Decentralisation – Why and How to Make it Work, The Handelsbanken Way*, Kristianstad 2003 [Swedish original: Kristianstad 2002].

Walters, Brian: *The Fall of Northern Rock*, Petersfield 2008.

Note: All the books above are available for purchase at
books.global-investor.com.

Index

A

B

D

E

F

J

K

L

V

W